THE WESTERN CONCEPT OF INDIVIDUALISM AND ITS IMPACT ON THE GHANAIAN SOCIETY

A SOCIAL PHILOSOPHICAL PERSPECTIVE

REV. FR. DR. JOHN DOE DORMAH

The Western Concept of Individualism and its
Impact on the Ghanaian Society
A Social Philosophical Perspective

Paperback ISBN: 978-1-952982-69-9
Ebook ISBN: 978-1-952982-70-5

Published by Green Sage Agency   01/19/2021

Green Sage Agency
1-888-366-9989
inquiry@greensageagency.com

CONTENTS

DEDICATION

This work is dedicated to my mother Felicia Akua Attah and all who work hard for the individual to be valued and accepted in every society as a person.

PREFACE

The idea to write this book began when I was writing my dissertation for a doctorate degree in philosophy. After studying philosophy, I asked myself this basic question: How can all the knowledge I have acquired be used to help humanity? Coming from Ghana, a country in West Africa, I realised the hardship people go through just to make ends meet, and how society has ignored the welfare of the individual. I therefore decided to use the knowledge I have acquired to empower the individual. And this is what I have been doing for more than a decade now. I have the strong conviction that, given equal opportunities, the individual has all that it takes to succeed.

The work thus centres on how the Western concept of individualism as a social philosophical thought system has influenced and continues to influence the individual in the Ghanaian society today. The work concentrates on the impact of this concept of the individual in his society so far as social, political, economic, and religious life is concerned. According to the definition of the *New Oxford Dictionary*, the "individual" refers to the single human being distinct from a group, a class or family. This work brings into consideration the welfare of the individual which is being neglected in Ghana today.

Below are the trajectories through the various chapters of the book. They give a glimpse of the content of the book to the reader.

Chapter 1: The Empowerment of the Individual by Western Philosophy from Late Antiquity till Date. In this chapter, I have given to the reader the imprint and how the individual was perceived from late antiquity till date. Through these epochs one will see the individual as a concept and reality which develops and evolves, thereby empowering the various epochs. Individuals have empowered themselves based on what they experienced and understood about individualism in these times. Philosophers of the epoch have defined and redefined what the individual is and ought to be.

Chapter 2: The Concept of Individualism in Social Philosophy. Here the concept and the emergence of individualism are expressed. I have also delineated what the individual is not and the features of individualism. Concerning individualism and civic society, I have presented the work of some philosophers like Thomas Hobbes, John Locke, and Jean-Jacques Rousseau to enlighten the individual. The concepts of these philosophers provide insight on how the individual is related to the civic society to which he belongs. The individual is naturally linked to and in a close relationship with the society.

Chapter 3: The Tribal System in Ghana and the Individual. In this chapter, looking at the indigenous Ghanaian concept of the individual, I have expressed through the Ghanaian lens how the individual is shaped and empowered. This chapter talks about how the community including the clan, family, and religion shape the conception of the individual in Ghana. In this chapter, the reader gets to know that the individual is empowered or disempowered by beliefs typical of the Ghanaian. The clan, family, and religion shape the individual to fit into these areas of the Ghanaian tribal system.

Chapter 4: The Encounter with the West. After a twist in chapter three concerning the Ghanaian context and the individual, in this chapter, I introduce the reader to an encounter with the West. The empowerment of the individual in the first chapter is from the Western perspective and there is the need to know how the encounter with the West builds up the individual. The encounter that the individual in traditional society had with the West from antiquity till date ranges from trade, the process of colonization, missionary activities through to globalization. These encounters empower the individual to know his history and forge ahead to be a better person or individual. Talking about our encounter without these elements will be futile. The individual must look back on these encounters and either pick up the pieces of the self or individual or improve upon himself and see the way forward.

Chapter 5: The Individual in the Ghanaian Society Today. Looking at the concept of the individual through the spectra of the West and the Ghanaian contexts, there is the need to know what the individual is in the Ghanaian society today. The individual cannot evolve without facing crises. The crises can batter him, as he is confronted with a new economic life, political life, and socio-cultural life. But these crisis situations build him up and empower him to be a better person.

As a priest and lecturer, I have been able to motivate my congregations and students with this ideology. I have decided to publish this work in order to satisfy the unending request for me to pen down some of my thoughts so that future generations and people from all over the world can benefit from it. This is the much awaited book and anyone who reads it will be empowered to achieve his life goals. This piece is recommended for all and sundry because it brings out the real meaning and encompasses all there is to know about the individual.

Rev. Fr. Dr. John Doe Dormah

ACKNOWLEDGEMENTS

"Commit your care unto the Lord, trust in him and he will act." (Ps. 37: 5)

I wish to express my largess of heart to Professor Dr. Erwin Bader of the Department of Social Philosophy of the Faculty of Philosophy in the University of Vienna for his concern, support, understanding and inspiration. I am also grateful to Professor Dr. Franz Wimmer of the University of Vienna who inspired me a great deal with his articles on Africa. I am grateful to Dr Markus Riedenauer also of the University of Vienna for his help. I am also grateful to Professor Dr. Ingerboug Gabriel and Dr. B. Taubald of the Social Ethics Department of the Faculty of Catholic Theology of the University of Vienna for their inspirations. My heartfelt gratitude goes to Most Rev. Francis A.K Lodonu, Bishop Emeritus of the Ho Diocese in Ghana for giving me the opportunity to further my studies. I wish to thank the Augustinian Chorherrenstift Klosterneurburg for their brotherly love and care. I am equally grateful to the Archdiocese of Vienna for giving me the chance to continue with my pastoral work alongside my studies. My appreciation also goes to the Austrian government for granting me a scholarship for my studies. My special thanks also go to my mothers, Felicia Atta and Susana Ablekpe for their love and their moral support. I also thank Dr. Streit, Madam Elisabeth Markus, Franz Nowak, Rev. Fr. Prof. Michael Perry Kweku Okyerefo, Rev. Fr. Dr. Emmanuel Richard Mawusi, Rev. Fr. Dr. Paul Agbodza and all those who in one way or the other helped me in the course of my studies and have made this book a possibility. God bless you all.

I am grateful to the following for their recommendations; Rev. Fr. Dr. Francis Arthur, Rev. Fr. Paul A. Agbodza (PhD), Rev. Fr. Dr. Joseph Okine-Quartey, Professor Emmanuel Debrah, Louis Doe Atsiatorme (PhD) and Dr. Raphael Avornyo.

Special thanks go to Rev. Fr. Professor Michael Perry Kweku Okyerefo, Dean, School of Arts, University of Ghana for writing the *FOREWORD*. Specials thanks also go to Dr. Raphael Avornyo for accepting to look at the manuscript and making useful suggestions. Indeed, Dr. Raphael was instrumental in looking at the editorial and proofreading aspects of this book.

RECOMMENDATIONS

The individual is a product of various encounters and experiences. Just as the various facets of our society are shaped by Western concepts and thoughts, the individual in Ghana is no exception of this encounter with the West. *THE WESTERN CONCEPT OF INDIVIDUALISM*

AND ITS IMPACT ON THE GHANAIAN SOCIETY: A SOCIAL PHILOSOPHICAL PERSPECTIVE gives a repertoire which the individual needs to encounter his or her real self through the lens of Ghanaian empowerment. By reading this book, the individual is poised to comprehend the self not only through the Western perspective but through the very webs of the Ghanaian context. Read it to empower and encounter the new and real *YOU!*

REV. FR. DR. FRANCIS ARTHUR

Former Rector, St. Paul's Catholic Seminary, Sowutuom

In his book, *THE WESTERN CONCEPT OF INDIVIDUALISM AND ITS IMPACT ON THE GHANAIAN SOCIETY: A SOCIAL PHILOSOPHICAL PERSPECTIVE*, Dr. Dormah addresses a core feature of human nature, 'the need for self-preservation'. This is exhibited in individualism. While this need is required for survival, its extreme utilization disadvantages and robs significant others of their living space. In the book, one can catch the glimpse of a feature of contemporary culture demonstrated by the advent of mobile devices. The thesis here is "prophetic".

REV. FR. PAUL A. AGBODZA, PhD

The individual is a fundamental building block of society. From the times of Thales through Descartes to Gyekye, the individual's identity has shifted from acting without following the in-group through the melting pot effect to the salad bowl effect. In that salad bowl of the social order, the individual, acting without sacrificing his God-given identity, acts so as to promote mutuality of respect and collaborative spirit. Dr. Dormah drives home the idea of the individual's self-realization in regards to society and social changes.

In a chronology of philosophical thoughts, he offers a global view and a useful resource for undergraduate and graduate search into the concept of the human person as an individual and the impact society has on him or her. The blend of western philosophical thought with traditional African thought is splendid. The individual is a bundle of every experience he makes in his or her micro and macrocosm as a social being. No individual is a finished business. Through socio-cultural changes, the individual amid inner conflicts constantly reforms the self and his or her identity.

REV. FR. DR. JOSEPH OKINE-QUARTEY

Former Academic Dean, St. Paul's Catholic Seminary, Sowutuom.

This is an excellent piece of work, a unique exemplar of the value of bringing together historical narrative, philosophical insight and empirical vigour to illuminate our understanding of how the individual has functioned both in antiquity and contemporary complex society. This book is highly recommended for students of philosophy, sociology and history.

PROFESSOR EMMANUEL DEBRAH

Former Head, Department of Political Science and currently, Director, Legon Centre for International Affairs and Diplomacy, University of Ghana, Legon.

The individual is nurtured within a culture milieu and the process can be complex and in fact it is complex. This process is or can become a strong determinant of who the individual will become. Working with people or ministering to people requires understanding and improvement of self within the context of the individual's culture. Fr. Dormah presents a comprehensive, consistent and a coherent analysis of the process of nurturing of the individual within a culture milieu in his book, *THE WESTERN CONCEPT OF INDIVIDUALISM AND ITS IMPACT ON THE GHANAIAN SOCIETY: A SOCIAL PHILOSOPHICAL PERSPECTIVE.* The book helps the reader to understand this complex process within the context of western education and religion, the understanding which can lead to the improvement of self. It is a MUST read book.

LOUIS DOE ATSIATORME (PhD)

Director, Africa Center for Environment Management and Education, Ghana

Johann Wolfgang von Goethe, the famous German literary figure, once said: "The person born with a talent they are meant to use will find their greatest happiness in using it" and Derek Jeter, the American former professional baseball shortstop, businessman, and baseball executive said: "There may be people who have more talent than you, but there is no excuse for anyone to work harder than you do – and I believe". What these two quotes indicate is that by making use of their talents every individual can achieve his or her goals in life. But how do we discover our talents?

In *THE WESTERN CONCEPT OF INDIVIDUALISM AND ITS IMPACT ON THE GHANAIAN SOCIETY: A SOCIAL PHILOSOPHICAL PERSPECTIVE*, the author has provided us with an impeccably researched work for all our questions regarding the ability of the individual to discover his or her talents and attain his or her life goals.

Rev. Fr. Dr. John Doe Dormah has carried out a thorough research on the concept of individualism in all human societies, including that of Ghana. The book is of high relevance and offers a very important source of empowerment for all individuals, particularly those in sub-Saharan Africa, to develop themselves and contribute to the growth of their societies.

DR. RAPHAEL AVORNYO

FOREWORD

The individual and society are two complex concepts, which have been under scrutiny and interpretation throughout different epochs of history. Of interest is how the agencies and social interactions of individuals create societies while the resultant societies at the same time constrain and liberate the individual. Philosophers and social scientists continue to be preoccupied with debates surrounding this reality with the cross-fertilization of ideas of thinkers in the various fields. Greek philosophers are credited to have laid the foundation of the various trajectories of philosophical thinking about the individual and society. At the same time, however, one must not forget the pioneering role of the African Ibn Khaldun in developing the study of social interaction or society, which we refer to as sociology today.

Drawing on the theories and concepts under-pinning the ongoing debate regarding the 'individual-as-actor' who constructs his or her own biography or the individual as 'self-integrated in a web of social and historical relations' that influence him or her, the Rev. Fr. (Dr.) John Doe Dormah proffers an integral course for the individual.

In his book, *The Western Concept of Individualism and Its Impact on the Ghanaian Society: A Social Philosophical Perspective*, the author, by means of the tool of dialectical development, helps the reader appreciate the concept of individualism from both Western and Ghanaian perspectives. The 'uncertain individual' is given a tool for growth and cultural appreciation. Not only is the reader (as the individual in question) made to understand the concept of individualism as a subject matter for all who want to understand the self, the author gives a recipe for deconstructing a myth that it is only the business of scholars who possess a complete understanding of the individual.

The Western Concept of Individualism and Its Impact on the Ghanaian Society: A Social Philosophical Perspective seeks to guide the perplexed on how the individual can encounter his or her society, in this case the Ghanaian society, through the appreciation of philosophy, history and culture. By means of the historical narrative method, the Reverend Father Dormah rallies the individual to reflect on Ghanaian culture and its influence on the development of the individual.

As both creators and products of society, individuals are the epicenters of this dynamic. That is why, in spite of the enormous influence Western society and its conceptualization exerts on Ghanaian culture, the book argues that it is important for the individual to confront its containment while engaging with concepts, such as individualism in one's own culture and its liberating effect on the self.

This book is timely in an age where the individual is in dire need of a sense of direction and purpose through closer realization of a true self.

MICHAEL PERRY KWEKU OKYEREFO

Cultural Sociologist & Sociologist of Religion; Dean, School of Arts, University of Ghana.

INTRODUCTION

A quick look at the political, economic, and social situation in our world today can easily show that ideologies, theories, concepts, principles and so on, have not solved the world's problems as expected. One gets the impression that these ideologies, theories, concepts and principles meant to make life easy for the ordinary individual tend to benefit a cross section of the society at the expense of the other. What this work set out to do was to look at how the Western concept of individualism as a social philosophical thought system has and continues to influence the individual in the Ghanaian society today. The work will concentrate on the impact of this concept of the individual on society so far as social, political, economic, and religious life is concerned. Hence the thesis statement of this work is: The Western social philosophical concept of individualism has and continues to influence the individual in the Ghanaian society today. How far is this statement tenable?

The word 'individual' is defined by the *New Oxford Dictionary* as a single human being distinct from a group, a class or family. The etymology of the word is from the Latin word *individuus* meaning *in* as 'not' and *dividuus* meaning 'divisible'. So the word individual simply put means *that which cannot be divided.*

For Aristotle, the ordinary individual is ontologically basic. He is a rational animal, a substance differentiated from another individual only by accident. Adler (1956) found the individual to be *"a self-consistent unity"* understood as a unity that brings together the various aspects of the individual - his thinking, feeling, acting in his conscious and unconscious mind, and in every expression of his personality. For him, **we can understand the parts only through the total.**

Looking at Ghana today, one can observe that the people are struggling day in and day out in order to make ends meet. Even the seemingly rich people are under some kind of pressure. The politicians are at their wits' end. The traditional system of maintaining harmony is only struggling to survive. Society and its structures do not seem to take the welfare of the individual into consideration. Economic progress seems to be at the expense of the environment. Many people continue to experience, in a rather extreme manner, economic hardships. Political power is no more at the service of the community. Money and wealth seem to be the only means by which one's status in society is measured. The just watch in dismay how justice and fame are being commercialised. Moral values are at the verge of collapse. As social vice continues to rise, the people are becoming aggressive day in, day out; many of them look frustrated and some have even resigned to fate.

Over the years, attempts have been made to rescue this deteriorating situation. Governments have been changed; programs have been drawn and redrawn to recover the economy and to rescue traditional values in order to give some hope and security to the individual. But the majority of Ghanaians live and continue to live in misery. They are without social security, quality health services, good education, and economic prosperity. As the former family security becomes threatened, there is fear for the future, a kind of confusion. What happens to the youth who migrate to the cities in search of white colour job? In the face of these situations, some scholars are calling for a return to the old system of simplicity. Others think development can only be effective from the Western civilisation point of view. Where lies the remedy? Has individualism as a concept anything to offer or has it confused the individual Ghanaian as long as his membership of the society is concerned?

To reach a conclusion, the work will start in the first chapter with a *dialectical development* of the concept of the individual from late antiquity through the medieval period to the renaissance. It will continue with the 16th century and 17th century developments to the 18th century Enlightenment and the period after Enlightenment. The purpose of this chapter is to see the philosophy behind the individual as the most important object of nature. The second chapter will look at individualism as a philosophical concept and how the individual's social, political, economic, and religious life is affected. In the third chapter, we shall then divert our attention to Ghana to see the concept of the individual and its relationship to family life, society, economic prosperity, the transcendental, morality and life after death.

The fourth chapter will show how Ghana came into contact with the West, ending up in colonialism. Here, the impact of this encounter on the individual and his society will be discussed. The fifth chapter will look at the situation as it is today and what schools of thought or camps exist and the ideas that are being proposed to give value to the individual as a citizen of Ghana.

CHAPTER ONE

THE EMPOWERMENT OF THE INDIVIDUAL BY WESTERN PHILOSOPHY FROM LATE ANTIQUITY TILL DATE

Introduction

The desire of many scholars to understand human nature and contribute towards making life better for the individual cannot be overemphasized. This has moved many scholars to devote their time in studying the individual. Among others, one feels that he comes to know human nature through *the character* and *conduct of other individuals* he meets. Behind what they do, one recognizes qualities that often are not surprising. Human beings are proud, sensitive, eager for recognition or admiration, often ambitious, hopeful or despondent, and selfish or capable of self-sacrifice. They take satisfaction in their achievements, feel guilty and are loyal or disloyal, to mention but a few. Experience in dealing with and observing people give rise to a conception of a predictable range of conduct. Conduct falling outside the range that is considered not to be worthy of an individual is frequently regarded as inhuman or bestial, whereas that which is exceptional in that it lives up to standards, which most people recognize, but few achieve is regarded as superhuman or saintly. Thus, the common conception of human nature implicitly locates man on a scale of perfection, placing him somewhere above most animals but below angels.

Two sayings that have been adopted as mottoes by those who see themselves as engaged in philosophical study of the individual date from the 5th century BC. These are: "***Man is the measure of all things***" stated by Protagoras and "***Know thyself***", a saying from the Delphic oracle that was echoed by Heraclitus, Socrates, among others. Both sayings reflect a specific orientation of philosophical anthropology as humanism, which takes man as its starting point and treats man as the centre or origin, on which all other disciplines ultimately depend (Encyclopaedia Britannica, 1994-2001).

What this chapter is out to consider is the dialectical empowerment of the individual by Western philosophy over the centuries. We shall start by looking at how some of the classical Greek philosophers looked at how the individual emancipates from attributing everyday happening to the forces of nature to the use of reason. We shall then look at how the individual is seen in the medieval period, the Renaissance, the Reformation, the 16th and 17th centuries, the 18th century Enlightenment and the period after Enlightenment. The aim of this is to bring out in clear terms the efforts made over the years in placing the individual over and above every other thing, and also making him the most important being without which nothing has worth.

Late Antiquity

Western philosophy is considered generally to have begun in ancient Greece. Philosophy among the Greeks slowly emerged out of *religious awe into wonder about the principles and elements of the natural world*. Eventually, cosmological speculation partly gave way to moral and political theorizing. As the Greek populations left the land to become concentrated in their cities, interest shifted from nature to social living and so questions of law and convention and civic values became paramount. Among other things, it is believed that the *Ionian school* made the initial radical step from mythological to scientific explanation of natural phenomena. Mythology is here understood to be *a symbolic narrative usually of unknown origin and at least partly traditional, that apparently relates actual events associated with religious belief*. It is distinguished from symbolic behaviour (cult, ritual) and symbolic places or objects (temples, icons). They are simply specific accounts of gods or superhuman beings involved in extraordinary events or circumstances in a time that is unspecified but which is understood as existing apart from ordinary human experience.

Ross (Encyclopaedia Britannica, 1994-2001) explains that the way the pre-philosophical individual thought could be characterized as *"mythopoeic," "mythopoetic,"* or *"mythic"* thought. He went on to explain *"Mythopoeic"* to mean *"making"* and *"myth"* (**mûthos)** i.e. stories about persons, where persons may be gods, heroes, or ordinary people. Differentiating myth from philosophy, he identified that myths by their nature are conservative, not argumentative. They allow for a multiplicity of explanations which are not logically exclusive. In other words, they can contradict each other, and are often humorous. We identify the pre-philosophic individual as one that looked up almost solely to supernatural powers for solution to problems. He did that by means of stories. In other words, myths were not founded on any scientific proof, but were all the same important for his survival, because they gave him answers to questions he could not answer; they gave him security and maintained order and stability in the community (Ross, 1946).

Ruano (n. d.), writing about Rudolf Steiner, states that he thinks *that the individual even at this pre-philosophic level wishes to stand at the topmost place in the world, however, he does not dare to pronounce himself the pinnacle of creation*. Therefore he invents gods in his own image and lets the world be ruled by them. He thinks that the religious person cannot set himself up as the lord of the world, but he does indeed determine, out of his own absolute power, the likes and dislikes of the ruler of the world. This explains why even though there are countless people who believe themselves governed by gods, there are none who do not independently, over the heads of the gods, judge what pleases or displeases these gods. Thus, we can conclude that no matter how unclear the individual was at this time about his relationship to the world, he nevertheless seeks within himself the yardstick by which to measure all things. Out of a kind of unconscious feeling of sovereignty he decides on the absolute value of all happenings. *It is worth mentioning that philosophy or reason did not set in to take the place of mythological thought. All it did was to find a reasonable or logical meaning to what the individual could not explain unless with the help of supernatural powers and myths.* What we realise is that with philosophy the individual decided not to live in the chance proximity into which nature has placed him, hence he seeks to regulate the way he lives with others in accordance with his reason.

The transition from the mythological thinking into philosophical thinking is particularly interesting. Here thinkers in the persons of Thales, Anaximander, Heraclitus, and Parmenides will be of interest. In Thales we see the individual approaching the world in an entirely free way. His way of thinking is no longer religious at all. When we accept the emphasis by Hegel that **thinking is the trait, which distinguishes man from the animals**, then we shall see **Thales** as the first Western personality who dared to assign to thinking its sovereign position. Man only knew that he thought, and assumed that, because he thought, he also had a right to explain the world to himself in accordance with his thinking, a clear disregard for all religious preconceptions. One sees here a declaration of the absoluteness of human thinking. Man thinks about the world, and by virtue of his thinking he ascribes to himself the power to judge the world (Steiner, 1989). Beginning with Thales therefore we can agree with Steiner (1989) that *the activity of knowing - das Erkennen -* now enters into a completely new stage of its development. Like Thales, it is clear that Anaximander no longer speaks of gods as his Greek ancestors did. For him the highest principle, which rules the world, is not a being pictured in man's image. It is an impersonal being, the *apeiron, the indefinite* (Russell, 1979). This develops out of itself everything occurring in nature, not in the way a person creates, but rather out of natural necessity.

For **Anaximander**, everything in the world occurs just as necessarily as a magnet attracts iron, but does so according to morality, i.e., human laws. Only from this point of view could he say: "*Whence things arise, hence must they also pass away, in accordance with justice, for they must do penance and recompense because of unrighteousness in a way corresponding to the order of time.*" This is the stage at which we identified the individual as being able to judge philosophically. He lets go of the gods. He no longer ascribes to the gods what comes from man. **Heraclitus** was of the view that all things are in eternal flux; that becoming is the essential being of things. This thought culminated in the popular statement; "*you cannot step in the same river twice*". When I step into a river, it is no longer the same one as in the moment of my deciding to enter it. This may be seen as an attempt to think out the causes of change in nature, and in man. We see **Parmenides** setting himself in absolute opposition to Heraclitus. With all the one-sidedness possible only to a keen philosophical nature, he rejected all testimony brought by sense perception. For, it is precisely this ever-changing sense world that leads one astray into the view of Heraclitus. Parmenides therefore regarded those revelations as the only source of all truth, which well forth from the innermost core of the human personality, the revelations of thinking. In his view, the real being of things is not what flows past the senses, it is the thoughts, the ideas that thinking discovers within this stream and to which it holds fast. He sees thought as the only means by which being is determined and that belongs to the individual (Audi, 1999).

What is impressive here, to begin with, is not at all whether the above mentioned persons believed water or anything else to be the principle of the world; what matters is that the individual says to himself: ***what the principle is, the individual person will decide by thinking***. There is *argument*, there is *disagreement*, there is *agreement*, there is a *challenge*, and there is a *proof*. The role of providence, fate, and the like are relegated to the background. We begin to admire an individual who begins to look for solutions in the causes of event by use of reason. If the gods are responsible, he will like to know to what extent. The individual questioned and tried to answer the question. By the time of Plato and Aristotle things had become clear. The individual's dependence on forces of nature was becoming a thing of the past. They became concerned with the composition and the potentials in the individual.

Their view of the individual was a consequence of their differing metaphysical views.

Plato's metaphysics was *dualistic*, claiming that the everyday physical world of changeable things, which man comes to know by the use of his senses, are not the primary reality but is a world of appearances or phenomenal manifestations, of an underlying timeless and unchanging reality, an immaterial realm of forms that is knowable only by use of the intellect. The ideal world, the inner representations that arise around man within his spirit while his gaze is directed, of which are the multiplicity of outer things, becomes for Plato a higher world of existence that multiplicity is only a copy. For him the things of this world, which our senses perceive, have no true being at all. *They are always becoming but never are.* They have only a relative existence and so in their totality, they are only in and through their relationship to each other. One can, therefore, call their whole existence a non-existence. They are consequently also not objects of any actual knowledge. For, only about what is, in and for itself and always in the same way, can there be such knowledge. So long as we are limited only to our perception of them, we are like people who sit in a dark cave so firmly bound that they cannot even turn their heads, hence they see nothing, except, on the wall facing them, by the light of a fire burning behind them, the shadow images of real things which are led across between them and the fire. Their wisdom, however, would be to predict the sequence of those shadows which they have learned to know from experience (*What is Really Real?*).

The individual for him is therefore in a prison-house, the world of sight, making a journey upward, ascent of the soul into the intellectual world. The building that I see and touch is therefore the shadow of the idea of the house. And this idea is what is truly real. The idea, however, is what lights up within my spirit when I look at the house. What I perceive with my senses is thus made into a copy of what my spirit shapes through the perception. This is the view expressed in the *Republic* in his celebrated *Metaphor of the Cave*, where the changeable physical world is likened to shadows cast on the wall of a cave by graven images. To know the real world the occupants of the cave must first turn around and face the graven images in the light that casts the shadows and, secondly, must leave the cave to study the originals of the graven images in the light of day. Similarly, human bodily existence is merely an appearance of the true reality of the human being. The conclusion we can draw from this is that *the identity of a human being does not derive from the body but from the character of his or her soul, which is an immaterial entity.* There is thus a divorce between the rational and the material aspects of human existence, one in which the material is devalued. (Russell, 1979, pp. 66-70). *"Plato therefore maintained the ultra-dualism of body and soul (mind). The body is a material substance, and the soul is a spiritual substance. The two substances form a dynamic unit, but not a substantial unit"* (Plato, *Republic* Book VII).

Aristotle did not agree with Plato on this. He insisted that the physical, changeable world made up of concrete individual substances is the primary reality. For him *each* *individual substance may be considered to be **a composite of matter and form**, but these components are not separable, for the forms of changeable things have no independent existence.* They exist only when materially instantiated. This general metaphysical view, then, undercut Plato's body-soul dualism. Aristotle synthesized body and mind by assuming that the soul of man is the formal, organizing, animating principle of primal matter. For Aristotle, all things had each a unique *"Form"* which gave it its distinct existence as a particular entity. Thus a Human Form gave human potential its existence as a particular person, and this forms such a person as an individual. This is also responsible for particular instincts of this person; the constant desire to move forward toward some sense of personal *"potential,"* or *"not-yet-realized existence"*. For Aristotle, all life was a process of moving toward one's potential, something like a life-giving struggle to realize one's self fully. The soul is the form of the body, giving life and structure to the specific matter of a human being. For him all human beings are the same in respect to form and therefore their individual differences are to be accounted for by reference to the matter in which this common form is variously instantiated. This being so, it is impossible for an individual human soul to have any existence separate from the body. Matter and soul are therefore two incomplete substances or substantial co-principles, and their union results in a single, unitary substance, namely, the human organism. Thus, while safeguarding body and mind (soul) as distinct realities, he gives a neat explanation of their synthesis into one substance

The period of Greek thought that follows Plato and Aristotle concerns itself with the individual wish to attain happiness. It announces itself with the *Stoics* and *Epicureans* and reaches its high point with the *skeptics*. The Stoics and Epicureans feel instinctively that one cannot find the essential being of things along the path taken by their predecessors. They were concerned with how man should live his life. Everything else was only a means to this end. According to Audi (1999, pp. 269-270), the Stoics considered all philosophy to be worthwhile if through it man could know how he is to live his life. For them the right life for man is one that is in harmony with nature. In order to realize this harmony with nature in one's own actions, one must first know what is in harmony with nature. We see in Stoics' teachings an important admission about the human personality, namely that ***the human personality can be its own purpose and goal and that everything else, even knowledge, is there only for the sake of this personality***.

According to Audi (1999, pp. 879-881), the Epicureans went even further in this direction. Their striving consisted in shaping life in such a way that man would feel as content as possible in it or that it would afford him the greatest possible pleasure. One's own life stood so much in the foreground for them that they practiced knowledge only for the purpose of freeing man from superstitious fear and from the discomfort that befalls him when he does not understand nature. Thus a heightened human feeling of oneself runs through the views of the Stoics and Epicureans compared to those of older Greek thinkers. This view appears in a finer, more spiritual way in the skeptics (Audi, 1999, pp. 846-850). They were convinced that when an individual is forming ideas about things, he could form them only out of himself. And only out of himself can he draw the conviction that an idea corresponds to something. They saw nothing in the outer world that would provide a basis for connecting thing and idea. And they regarded as delusion and combated what anyone before them had said about any such bases. The basic characteristic of the Skeptical view could be regarded as modesty. Its adherents did not dare to deny that there is a connection in the outer world between idea and thing; they merely denied that man could know of any such connection. Therefore, they did indeed make man the source of his knowing, but they did not regard this knowing as the expression of true wisdom. Thus, so far we see the course of development taken by Greek thinking lying between the two extremes of naive, blissful confidence in man's cognitive ability and absolute lack of confidence in it. In the period that followed, they tried to reconcile the individual with the supernatural world through Christian religion.

Medieval Period

Bader (1991) states that Christianity is the historical foundation of Europe. He explains that even though Christianity has suffered at various stages of European history, the Christian religion remains the only institution, which has survived ideologies and wars (Bader, 1991, pp.16-17). The Christian Church, and for that matter Christianity, dominated Western medieval culture. This influence was naturally reflected in the philosophy of the period. ***Theology, rather than metaphysics, tended to be given primacy***, even though many of the structures of Greek philosophy, including its metaphysics were preserved.

In the light of this metaphysics, form and matter was readily assimilated into Christian thought. Forms became ideas in the mind of God, the patterns according to which he created and continues to sustain the universe. Christian theology, however, modified the positions, requiring some sort of compromise between *Platonic* and *Aristotelian* views. We see the creation story in the Bible making the individual a creature among other creatures, but not a creature like other creatures. The differentiation here must be noted; human beings are distinct from other creatures. The individual, being the product of the final act of divine initiative, was given responsibility for the Garden of Eden, and had the benefit of a direct relationship with his creator. The fall of man through Adam and redemption through Christ, the categories of sin and grace, are seen to concern only the descendants of Adam, who were given a nature radically different from that of the animals and plants over which they were given dominion. The individual alone can, after a life in this world, hope to participate in an eternal life that is far more important than the temporal life that he lives here. From what we have seen so far it became clear that belief in a life after death makes it impossible to regard the individual as wholly a natural being. It also entails that the physical world now inhabited by the individual is not the sole, or even the primary reality. Yet, the characteristically Christian doctrine of the resurrection of the body also entails that the human body cannot be regarded as being of significance only in the mortal, physical world.

In line with the above Christian philosophy, the teachings of St. Augustine "gave prominence to Platonic views. "Augustine's God is a wholly immaterial, supremely rational and transcendent creator of the universe" (Encyclopaedia Britannica, 1994-2001). For Augustine, *the soul is not the entire man but his better part.* There remains a Platonic tendency to regard the body as a prison for the soul and a mark of man's fallen state. The emphasis he came to place on the significance of free will was one of the important consequences of Augustine's own pursuit of these two endeavours. He believes that *"since the seat of the will was reason, when people exercise their will, they are acting in the image of God, the supreme rational being"*. On the other hand, Thomas Aquinas, whiles placing less emphasis on the will *"regarded the individual as acting in the image of God to the extent that he exercises and seeks to fulfil his intelligent nature"*. He, like Aristotle, rejected the Platonic tendency to devalue the body and insisted that it is part of the concept of the individual that he has flesh and bone, as well as a soul. It is interesting to note, however, that whatever line the argument on the relation between the mind and body may take, the view of the individual was that he was first and foremost a creature of God privileged by having been created in the image of God. The individual is *"given the gift of reason in virtue of which he also has free will* and must take the burden of moral responsibility for his own actions. In order to fulfil his distinctively human nature, man must thus order his thoughts and actions in such a way as to reflect the supremacy of religious values" (Grayling, 1998, pp. 523-525).

The Renaissance

As pointed out above, until the 15th century, the standard assumption was that *the individual had a fixed nature, one that determined both his place in the universe and his destiny.* The dominant intellectual movement of the period was Renaissance, whose philosophy of *humanism* was based on the idea that people are rational beings who possess within themselves the capacity for truth and goodness. It emphasized the dignity and worth of the individual. The humanists expressed an enormous confidence in the power of reason as a source of profound understanding of human nature and of our place in the natural order. Humanism displaced Scholasticism as the principal philosophy of Western Europe and deprived church leaders of the monopoly on learning that they had previously held (Grayling, 1998, pp. 549-551). The Renaissance humanists, however, proclaimed that ***what distinguishes the individual from all other creatures is that he has no nature***. This was a way of asserting that the individual's actions are not bound by laws of nature in the way that those of other creatures are. The individual is capable of taking responsibility for his own actions because he has the freedom to exercise his will. It was in this cultural context of the Renaissance, and in particular with the Italian humanists and their imitators, that *the individual, his nature,* and *his capacities and limitations* became a primary focus of philosophical attention. The individual did not thereby cease to view himself within the context of the world, nor did he deny the existence of God. He did, however, disengage himself sufficiently from the bonds of cosmic determination and divine authority to become a centre of interest in his own eyes.

In the period of the Renaissance one could say that the educated people of the West rediscovered a clear conscience instead of the guilty conscience of Christianity. At the same time, the great inventions and discoveries suggested that the individual could take pride in his accomplishments and regard himself with admiration. These themes of **the dignity** and **excellence of the individual** were prominent in Italian humanist thought and can be found clearly expressed in Giovanni Pico della Mirandola's influential work titled: *De hominis dignitate oratio (Oration on the Dignity of Man)*. In this work, Pico della Mirandola expresses a view of the individual person that breaks radically with Greek and Christian tradition. He thinks that *"what distinguishes man from the rest of creation is that he has been created without form and with the ability to make of himself what he will. Being without form or nature he is not constrained, fated, or determined to any particular destiny"* (Encyclopaedia Britannica, 1994-2001, n. p.). The individual is therefore given the chance to choose what he will become. In this way, man's distinctive characteristic becomes his freedom. One is therefore free to make himself in the *image of God* or in *the image of beasts*. This essentially optimistic view of the individual is believed to be a product of the revival of Neo-Platonist thought. Its optimism is based on a view that the individual is at least potentially a non-natural, godlike being. But this status is now one that must be earned. The individual must win his right to dominion over nature and in so doing earn his place beside God in the life hereafter. He must learn both about himself and about the natural world in order to be able to achieve this. This was, however, only one of two streams of humanist thought. The other, more Aristotelian, was essentially more pessimistic and skeptical, stressing the limitations on man's intellectual capacities. In this case, there is an insistence on the need to be reconciled to the fact of man's humanity rather than to persist in taking seriously his superhuman pretensions and aspirations.

The Reformation

The Reformation is seen as that great 16th century religious revolution, *which ended the ecclesiastical supremacy of the Pope in Western Christendom and resulted in the establishment of the Protestant churches*. Martin Luther, the German monk and theologian and father of the Reformation, was a radical reformer who condemned some of the basic teachings and practices of the Church (Encyclopaedia Britannica, 1994-2001). In their teachings, the reformers saw ***the individual before his maker as so helpless that he can only be saved by justification***. Pink (n. d.)explains this doctrine beautifully as "*a legal change from a state of guilt and condemnation to a state of forgiveness and acceptance, a change owed solely to a gratuitous act of God, founded upon the righteousness of Christ*" (Pink as quoted in Encyclopaedia Britannica, 1994-2001, n. p.). For him, the justification is an acceptance by which God receives us into His favour and esteems us as righteous persons. It is explained to consist in the remission of sins and the imputation of the righteousness of Christ... Justification, therefore, is no other than an acquittal from guilt of him who was accused, as though his innocence has been proved. Hooker (n. d.) thinks that "*The Freedom of the Christian*," is the theological and ideological core of Luther's thinking. The concept of "*freedom*" or "*liberty*" is the fundamental term of value, around which every other aspect of his thought rotates. He thinks that even though this is not our concept of freedom, in the eventual turn of time it gave rise to the notion of "***individual freedom***," and later "***political freedom***," and later "***economic freedom***". He asserts that following the Reformation most of the European Enlightenment revolved around freedom and the project of "liberating" people from false beliefs, false religion and arbitrary authority. He believes that this idea of "liberating" people, so common to the international politics of our own period, comes out of Luther's idea of freedom (Hooker, n. d. as cited in Encyclopaedia Britannica, 1994-2001, n. p.).

Bertrand Russell also sees the Reformation as a springboard for free thinking because in the absence of a hope for a unity in doctrine by the Protestants and the Catholics, there was an increase in men's freedom to think for themselves even about fundamentals (Pink, n. d.). In another development, received authority became subject to the probing of creative minds. The idea of the universe as a mechanism governed by a few simple laws that can be known had a subversive effect on the concepts of a personal God and individual salvation that were central to Christianity. Inevitably, the method of reason was applied to religion itself (Hooker, n. d. as cited in Encyclopaedia Britannica, 1994-2001, n. p.).

The 16th And 17th Centuries

In the period after the Reformation, the thought of Montaigne (1580) represented one of the first attempts at individual reflection. He explores the individual's different aspects in a spirit of empirical investigation that is freed from all ties to dogma. The earlier emphasis on man's humanity and on the limited nature of his capacities lead to a denial that he can, even by the use of reason, transcend the realm of appearances. It was proposed that the only form of knowledge available to him is experimental knowledge, gained in the first instance by the use of the senses. The effect of this skeptical move was twofold:

- The first effect was liberation from the claims of dogmatic authority to knowledge of a reality behind appearances and of moral codes based on them. Skeptical arguments were to the effect that human beings are so constituted that such knowledge must always be unavailable to them.

• The second effect was a renewal of attention to and interest in the everyday world of appearances, which now becomes the only possible object of human knowledge and concern.

In contrast to the above conception of the individual, we see in the works of the 17th century French philosopher, René Descartes (1596-1650), a continuation of the theme of optimism about men's capacities for knowledge. Descartes explicitly set out to beat the skeptics at their own game. He used their methods and arguments in order to vindicate claims to non-experimental knowledge of a reality behind appearances. In other words, the individual is capable of knowing what is beyond without experience. The *Meditations* thus begins with a turning in of Descartes upon himself but with the aim of finding there something that would go beyond the confines of his own mind. This inward journey was designed to show that each human being can come to knowledge of his intellectual self and that as he does so he will find within himself the idea of God, the mark of his creator, the mark that assures him of the existence of an objective order and of the objective validity of his rational faculties. Descartes no longer stood under the influence of Scholasticism. He recognized that the adherence of the Schoolmen to Christian teachings was only a matter of centuries-long habituation to these pictures. Therefore he considered it necessary first of all to doubt these habitual pictures and to seek a way of knowledge by which man can arrive at a kind of knowing whose certainty he does not assert out of habit, but which can be guaranteed at every moment through his own spiritual powers (Russell, 1979, p. 511).

Descartes had a strong feeling for the fact that man, through his thought-development, had brought himself into a perverted relationship with the world. Therefore, to begin with, he met everything that had come forth from this thought-development with doubt. Only when one doubts everything that the centuries have developed as truths can one, in his opinion, gain the necessary objectivity for a new point of departure.

In the process, one thing became clear to him; he could not doubt that he was doubting or thinking hence his classical statement *Cogito ergo sum* (*I think, therefore I am*) (Encyclopaedia Britannica, 1994-2001). Descartes presses even further. He is aware that the way man arrives at knowledge of himself should be a model for any other knowledge he means to acquire. *Clarity* and *definiteness* seem to Descartes to be the most prominent characteristics of self-knowledge. Therefore he also demands these two characteristics of all other knowledge. For him only that can stand as certain whatever man can distinguish just as clearly and definitely as his own existence. With this, the absolutely central place of the individual in the whole world is at least recognized in the area of cognitive methodology. Man determines the how of his knowledge of the world according to the how of his knowledge of himself, and no longer asks for any outer being to justify this how. He defended an ultra-dualism of body and soul in man. Regarding man's body, he advocated a *mechanistic atomism*; regarding man's soul, *ultra-spiritualism*. Man's ideas are potentially innate, not derived from sense data but through intellectual abstraction. Since man's mind can know only its own internal states, his theory of knowledge terminated in subjectivism, the theory which plagues practically all modern philosophy. The path Descartes took by starting with the individual and pressing forward to world knowledge is extended from now on by the philosophers of modern times.

For Steiner (1989), the Christian theological method, which had no confidence in the power of the individual as an organ of knowledge, was at least overcome. Like Descartes, the German philosopher, Leibniz, also recognized *the creative activity of the individual*. He had a very clear overview of the scope of this activity. He observed that it was inwardly consistent, and that it was founded upon itself. The individual for him is a world in itself, a *monad*. Only *monads*, i.e., beings creating out of and within them, exist. Each person is a world, a *monad*, in himself. He recognized that the individual is *active, creative*, within his inner being and so gives its content to itself and the individual brings this content into relationship with the other content of the world. This development of Western thought about the individual continues to manifest a very definite character in which the individual draws out of himself the best that he can know.

We see in George Berkeley a person for whom the creative being of the individual comes fully to consciousness. He had a clear picture of the individual's own activity in the coming about of all knowledge.

When I see an object, he said to himself, I am active. I create my perception for myself. The object of my perception would remain forever beyond my consciousness; it would not be there for me, if I did not continuously enliven its dead existence by my activity. I perceive only my enlivening activity, and not what precedes it objectively as the dead thing. No matter where I look within the sphere of my consciousness: everywhere I see myself as the active one, as the creative one (Encyclopaedia Britannica, 1994-2001, n. p.). In general, Descartes' *Cogito ergo sum* dominated this period even though there were those who still held on to the view that sense perception played a vital role in the individual's self-enlightenment.

The 18th Century Enlightenment

The Enlightenment is the term that has been retrospectively applied to the movement of advanced ideas in eighteenth century Europe and elsewhere. The 18th century Enlightenment saw a movement of thinkers who believed that science could explain everything in nature. Until then, most people believed that God controlled the universe in a "metaphysical" manner. A climate of relativism arose where patterns of behaviour and practices were considered as arbitrary customs rather than being endowed with inherent correctness. French writers compared their society with other European lands as well as distant countries. In this development, there was an enthusiastic study of the individual, as well as a growth of what would now be called Sociology. Writers disseminated their ideas in a variety of ways: *treatises, dialogues, travellers' tales, fiction* etc. Among others, people were encouraged to use science to explore nature and to question what they had always accepted without questioning. It encouraged people to participate in government and to rethink old ideas like feudalism and primogeniture.

The great German philosopher, Immanuel Kant, credited Hume for ***waking him up from his dogmatic slumbers***. But while Kant concurred with Hume in rejecting the possibility of taking metaphysics as a philosophical starting point (dogmatic metaphysics), he did not follow him in dismissing the need for metaphysics altogether. Instead he returned to the Cartesian project of seeking to find in the structure of consciousness itself something that would point beyond it. Thus, Kant started from the same point as the empiricists, but with Cartesian consciousness. *The experience of the individual he considered as a sequence of mental states.* But instead of asking the empiricists' question of how it is that man acquires such concepts as number, space, or colour, he enquired into the conditions under which the conscious awareness of mental states, as states of mind and as classifiable states distinguished by what they purport to represent, is possible. The empiricist simply takes the character of the human mind, consciousness, and self-consciousness for granted as a given of human nature and then proceeds to ask questions concerning how experience, presumed to come in the form of sense perceptions, gives rise to all of man's various ideas and ways of thinking. Even Hume was compelled to admit that self-observation, or introspection, given the supposed model of experience as a sequence of ideas and impressions, can yield nothing more than an impression of current or immediately preceding mental states. Experiential self-knowledge on this model is impossible. The knowing subject, by his effort to know himself, is already changing himself so that he can only know what he was, not what he is (Russell, 1979, p. 511).

Kant's position was firmly dualist; the conscious subject constitutes itself through the opposition between experience of itself as free and active (in inner sense) and of the thoroughly deterministic, mechanistic, and material world (in the passive receptivity of outer sense). The nature of man is not static and unalterable; the individual's own efforts to understand the world and adapt it to his needs, physical and spiritual, continuously transform that world and himself. Each individual is both the product and the support of a collective consciousness that defines a particular moment in the history of the human spirit (Steiner, 1989). Thus, with Kant we see the individual as possessing that knowledge that is indubitable. For Kant, the truths of pure mathematics and the general teachings of logic and physics seem to him to be in this category. In Kant's opinion, within the human soul there are certain principles present by which the manifoldness of sensations is brought into objective unities. Such principles are *space*, *time*, and certain connections such as *cause* and *effect*.

The contents of sensation are given to the individual but not their spatial interrelationships nor temporal sequence. Man first brings these to the contents of sensation. One content of sensation is given and another one also, but not the fact that one is the cause of the other. The intellect first makes this connection. Thus, there lie within the human soul, ready once and for all, the ways in which the contents of sensation can be connected. Thus, even though we can take possession of the contents of sensation only through experience, we can, nevertheless, before all experience, set up laws as to how these contents of sensation are to be connected. These laws are the ones given us within our own souls. We have, therefore, necessary kinds of knowledge. Therefore, the individual has a knowledge from experience and another, necessary, experience-free knowledge as to how the contents of experience can be connected. But we have no knowledge that goes beyond experience. Here one element does not come from outside and the other from within; both arise from a completely homogeneous content.

The philosophy of George Wilhelm Friedrich Hegel is a further bold attempt to explain the world on the basis of a content lying within the individual. According to Hegel, nature is nothing other than the content of the individual that has been spread out in space and time. Nature is this ideal content in a different state. "***Nature is spirit estranged from itself.***" Within the individual human spirit Hegel's stance toward the impersonal "I" is personal. Within self-consciousness, the being of the individual is not an *in*-itself, it is also for-itself; the human spirit discovers that the highest world content is his own content. This abstracting of everything personal manifests most strongly in Hegel's views about the spiritual life, the moral life. It is not the single, personal, individual "I" of man that can decide its own destiny, but rather it is the great, objective, impersonal world "I," which is abstracted from man's individual "I"; it is the general world reason, the world idea. The individual must submit to this abstraction drawn from its own being. Ludwig Feuerbach sought to put an end to this subordination by stating in powerful terms how man transfers his being into the outer world in order then to place himself over and against it, acknowledging, obeying, revering it as though it were a God. He advocated a general concept of a ***generic man***, and demands that *the individual should raise himself above the limitations of his individuality, because the individual is the function of the absolute as the absolute is a function of the individual* (Encyclopaedia Britannica, 1994-2001, n. p.)

The Period after Enlightenment

The philosophers of the Enlightenment agreed in thinking that the transcendence of God is doomed to fail by any attempt to encompass him within the framework of human discourse. But it became clear that with human truth – the only available truth – such a line was hard to maintain, and by the late 19th century the German philosopher Friedrich Nietzsche had announced that ***God was dead***. *But the death of God also meant that the essence of God in every man was dead.* Also dead was the part of a person that recognized universal God-given ideals of reason and truth, goodness and beauty. Here we have a view of an individual who, while integrating himself more thoroughly with the natural world, treating his incarnation as an essential aspect of his condition had to come to terms with the consequences of science and morality. The result is the removal of a transcendent support for belief in absolute standards or ideals. Thus the presumption of a fixed human nature was undercut at the level of natural history by the emergence and eventual acceptance of evolutionary biology. This made the individual a direct descendant of nonhuman primates and suggested that the gift of reason, which so many had seen as establishing a gulf between man and animal, might also have developed gradually and might indeed have a physiological basis. The evolutionary theory of Darwin (1859) is worth mentioning. In another development the experience of the Industrial Revolution was crucial to most 19th century concepts of the individual. There were those who saw in industrialization the progressive triumph of reason over nature, making possible the march of civilization and the moral triumph of reason over animal instinct. This was a view that continued the spirit of the Enlightenment, with its confidence in reason and the ability to advance through science.

The English philosopher John Stuart Mill, a stout defender of liberal individualism can be named among others. Mill's philosophy was in many respects a continuation of that of Hume but with the addition of Jeremy Bentham's utilitarian view that *the foundation of all morality is the principle that one should always act so as to produce the greatest happiness of the greatest number.* This ethical principle gives a prominent place to the sciences of man. Their studies were deemed necessary for an empirical determination of the social and material conditions that produce the greatest general happiness. This is a non-dialectical, naturalistic humanism, which gives primacy to the individual and stresses the importance of his freedom. For Mill, all social phenomena, and therefore ultimately all social changes, are products of the actions of individuals. Dissatisfied with the turn of affair as a result of the Industrial Revolution, the Romantics questioned the instrumental conception of the relation between man and nature, which is fundamental to the thinking behind much technological science. They insisted on an organic relation between the individual and the rest of nature. It is not the individual's place outside of nature that is emphasized but his situation within it. Karl Marx emphasized *the importance of labour and work in the individual's relation both to the natural and to the social worlds in which he finds himself and which condition his ability to realize himself.* He deplored the loss of humanity associated with capitalist industrialization, which was manifest in the alienating conditions under which members of the working class were treated as objects and thus deprived of their full status as human subjects by their industrial masters.

With Friedrich Nietzsche, we arrive at views that definitely lead to the path of absolute appreciation of the individual. In his opinion, genuine culture consists in fostering the individual in such a way that he has the strength out of himself to develop everything lying within him. Up until now, it was only an accident if an individual was able to develop himself fully out of himself. Nietzsche transfigured poetically, as his ideal, his type of man. He calls him *Übermensch* meaning *Superman*. He is man freed from all norms, who no longer wants to be the mere image of God, a being in whom God is well pleased, a good citizen, and so on, but rather who wants to be himself and nothing more — ***the pure and absolute egoist*** (Encyclopaedia Britannica, 1994-2001). Stirner (1993) demanded of the individual in a radical way that he finally recognizes that all the beings he has set above himself in the course of time were cut by him from his own body and set up in the outer world as idols. Every god, every general world reason, is an image of the individual and has no characteristics different from the individual. He calls upon man *to throw off everything general about himself and to acknowledge to himself that he is an individual.*

Steiner (1989, n. p.) quotes and explains how Stirner (1993) raises the individual above all categorization. *"You are indeed more than a Jew, more than a Christian, etc., but you are also more than a man. Those are all ideas; you, however, are in the flesh. Do you really believe, therefore, that you can ever become 'man as such'?"* I do not first have to produce man in myself, because he already belongs to me as all my characteristics do." "Only I am not an abstraction alone; I am the all in all... I am no mere thought, but I am at the same time full of thoughts, a thought-world. Hegel condemns what is one's own, what is mine ... 'Absolute thinking' is that thinking which forgets that it is *my* thinking, that *I* think, and that thinking exists only through me. As 'I,' however, I again swallow what is mine, am master over it; it is only my opinion that I can *change* at every moment, i.e., that I can destroy, that I can take back into myself and can devour." One can define everything else in the world by ideas, but we must *experience* our own "I" as something individual within us. "The individual is a word and with a word one would after all have to be able *to think* something; a word would after all have to have a thought-content. But the individual is a word *without thought;* it has no thought-content. This individual "I" can acknowledge no ethical obligation that it does not lay upon itself. "Whether what I think and do is Christian, what do I care? Whether it is human, liberal, humane, or inhuman, illiberal, inhumane, I don't ask about that. If it only aims at what I want, if I satisfy only myself in it, then call it whatever you like: it's all the same to me ..." "Perhaps, in the very next moment I will turn against my previous thought; I also might very well change my behaviour suddenly; but not because it does not correspond to what is Christian, not because it goes against eternal human rights, not because it hits the idea of mankind, humanity, humaneness in the face, but rather — because I am no longer involved, because I no longer enjoy it fully, because I doubt my earlier thought, or I am no longer happy with my recent behaviour" (Stirner, 1993, p.173 ff.).

We see from the above development that the individual will not allow anything to be determined for him by anything outside him. He wants to make himself into what he or she wants. Other writers of the late 19th and early 20th centuries that most influenced subsequent philosophical thought about the individual are Gottlob Frege, Edmund Husserl, Sigmund Freud and Alfred Adler, among others. For Frege, the individual participates in a rationality that is independent of him to the extent that he is a language user. He argued that if language is to be a vehicle for the expression of objective, scientific knowledge of the world, then the meaning (cognitive content) of a linguistic expression must be the same for all users of the language to which it belongs and must be determined independently of the psychological states of any individual.

Husserl, regarded as the founder of phenomenology, believed that laws of reasoning needed to be validated by reference to the objects of thought, but he did not agree that logic could be made purely formal and independent of the particular subject matter in hand, nor did he agree that the primary focus should be on language. He claimed, however, that all consciousness is intentional; in other words, one can only be conscious of something. The implication is that the individual can, in principle, abstract from every influence of culture and environment by abstracting also from that element of consciousness that involves awareness of self. It was presumed that consciousness as such had structures that would then be revealed. For Husserl, each individual is by necessity socially and historically conditioned by his environment.

Another important person worth mentioning as far as the individual is concerned is Sigmund Freud. He concerns himself with the mind of the individual and declares *that part of the mind that is accessible to consciousness is but the tip of a large iceberg.* The unconscious is the hidden remainder, which influences the conscious. Thus, for instance, there are unconscious desires that can cause someone to do things that he cannot explain rationally to others, or even to himself. In his later expositions, Freud assigned to the mind a tripartite structure consisting of the *id*, which contains all the instinctual drives seeking immediate satisfaction; the *ego*, which deals with the world outside the person, mediating between it and the id; and finally the *superego*, a special part of the ego that contains the conscience, the social norms acquired in childhood. Whatever can become conscious is in the ego, although even in it there may be things that remain unconscious, whereas everything in the id is permanently unconscious. The instincts or drives contained in the id are the motivating forces in the mental apparatus, and all of the energy of the mind comes from them. Freud also held that the first five or so years of life are the time in which the basis of an individual's personality is laid down. One cannot fully understand a person, therefore, until he comes to know the psychologically crucial facts about that person's early childhood (Encyclopaedia Britannica, 1994-2001, n. p.).

Adler (1956) presents us with the individual who aims only at an ultimate goal. He sees one basic dynamic force behind all human activities, *a striving from a felt minus situation towards a plus situation, from a feeling of inferiority towards superiority, perfection, totality.* This striving, he makes us to understand, receives its specific direction from an individually unique goal or self-ideal, which though influenced by biological and environmental factors, is ultimately the creation of the individual. The goal which is only "dimly envisaged" by the individual becomes the final cause, the ultimate independent variable that provides the key for understanding the individual.

For Adler (1956), the individual cannot be considered apart from his social situation. Because the individual is embedded in a social situation, social interest becomes crucial for his adjustment. Maladjustment is characterized by increased inferiority feelings, underdeveloped social interest, and an exaggerated uncooperative goal of personal superiority. Adlerian psychology adheres to the principle of affinity, expressed in the concept of goal. This goal has a starting point in a combination of factors found in early childhood. From what is inherited coupled by a thousand fold impressions given by his physique, his environment (people and surroundings), as well as the influences of climate, culture, and society, the child creates his very own way of survival and development. The chances are that he not merely is "on his way," but that he protects or defends himself in his very own way, and according to Adler (1956), with his "life style." Essential in Adlerian concept of the individual is the concept of creative ability. It is with his creative ability that the child tries to find his way in an unknown world, in which he has to find his place and has to achieve significance. Out of what is innate and what is outside of him, the individual, at an early age, creates his personal goal, which from there on dictates his actions, thinking, and feeling. Only if this personal goal is included in his concept of his significance can he become an integrated personality. This could be called the concept of overall-goal. For him every action serves a purpose. Both action and lack of action characterize the individual. If the individual has capacities, which he does not develop or use, his lack of action is typical for his life style. The basic thought is: 'Use' is more important than possession.

According to Adler (1956), there is not merely one way in which the individual can use what he has got; his creative ability is not limited to finding one certain combination out of what is innate and outside. He has choice, because as a human being he is capable of reasoning. If there were no choice, the individual would be inexorably submitted to his inheritance, environment, and the thousands of factors that influence his life; he would be entirely determined and therefore, never could use any creative ability. Whatever he might do would be determined by his fate. However, when we study life as it presents itself, we observe that man is capable of turning negative into positive. He may be found either on the negative or on the positive side of life as a result of the choice he makes out of all the possibilities. In order to justify his position on the negative side, it is important that he should not understand what he is doing so that ''unconsciously'' he can continue to follow his personal goal. For what may seem a storage place of obscure drives for which one cannot be responsible, the unconscious and subconscious, Adler (1956) coined the term "***the Un-understood***." It follows logically that Adlerian psychology uses a technique of *tolerance, patience*, and *encouragement*. The adult's insecurity and feelings of inadequacy are not very different from the child's. Both are facing difficulties for which they are not prepared. Nothing can objectively be a difficulty; we call a thing difficult as long as we don't know what to do about it. If we don't do anything at all, we turn the difficulty into a problem. According to Adlerian principles, mankind strives toward perfection. The individual, as part of mankind, has the inclination and at the same time has to accept his imperfection. Striving toward perfection with the acceptance of being imperfect leads toward improvement. This means that man is "on his way." (Stein, 1951, *Individual Psychology Bulletin*, Vol. 9). Another important philosopher who raises the individual above what is ordinary is Max Scheler, a German social and ethical philosopher, remembered for his phenomenological approach, after the philosophical method of the founder of phenomenology, Edmund Husserl. He differed from Husserl in his readiness to assign an independently real status to the objects. He and two other persons, namely Plessner and Gehlen, all of whom worked as sociologists, have some ideas in common. They include the aspiration to avoid the mind-body dualism (psychophysical neutral categories), the consideration of the social dimension of human life, without ignoring the organic nature of human beings. They nevertheless stress the ability of human beings to learn. In contrast to all animals, human beings do not live in their biological sphere, but rather in a world (*Welt*) they have constructed. This sphere is also called "second nature" or "culture" (*Kultur*).

Scheler (1928) identified the individual as the only one with what he calls the spirit (*Geist*) and life-urge (*Drang*). By itself, spirit is powerless, unless its ideas can "functionalize" with life-factors (material conditions) which allow their realization. Divine spirit also needs human life and history to become real. Utilizing the biological sciences, Scheler (1928) explores the ways in which human beings are like the rest of the biosphere. Humans, like other forms of life, have a psychic or life principle and are therefore "self-moving, self-differentiating and self-limiting in a spatial and temporal sense" and are not only objects for external observers but also have the quality of being in and for themselves with an inner life of their own. The approach of Scheler's (1928) philosophical anthropology is distinguished by his refusal to reduce the human *subject* to any *aspect* of the human being. Just as to speak of a human being without a body is nonsense, so it is nonsense to speak of a human being without a culture or without subjectivity. The factual reality is that all humans are biological and more-than-merely-biological beings. By reflecting on our actions we can experience ourselves as subjects and gain an "inner" and an "outer" knowledge of ourselves. We also have experiences of other individuals who are subjects and objects of action. This dynamic correlation of the interior and exterior aspects of an action in which two or more persons participate he referred to as "*intersubjectivity*" The structure of a human person's action, however, is the opposite of what we find in the rest of the animal world. Whereas in animals action and reaction are limited to and directed by biology and drives, human behaviour is motivated by *"a complex of sensations and ideas raised to the status of an object."* This difference has three important implications as follows:

i.   This ability of the individual to act; for an object raises the possibility that he or she can act independently and unlimited by the sensations he or she receives from the physical world.

ii. The individual can voluntarily release or inhibit his or her drives in response to the environment.

iii. The individual's action brings about a change both inside and outside of the acting individual.

He refers to this structure of human action as *"world-openness."* The human actor is self-conscious in and through his actions and thus knows himself as both a subject and an object. In the aiming of concentration at a goal we achieve self-consciousness. The individual, at the centre of his acts, can reflect on and objectify himself. This gives the individual the ability to be a subject, which has a centre, a unity of experience and action that can transcend different experiences and reflect on various sensations as a unity. By reference to their centre, persons are able to relate, coordinate and combine sensory data. This ability allows persons mastery over sensation and drives. Our ability to objectify our own body and our position in the environment enables us to have the world as an object because we are able to consider the world with ourselves abstracted.

As he puts it, man alone in so far as he is an individual is able to go beyond himself as an organism and transform, from a centre beyond the spatial-temporal world, everything (himself included) into an object of knowledge. In his view, the individual is able to "rise above" himself/herself as a living being. He portrays the human being as an "essence" supervening upon himself/herself and the world.

What we realize from the above is a capable individual who is a member of a society but one who neither allows himself to be dissolved into the society nor loses his identity. He is conscious of what he wants to achieve and struggles to achieve it by interpreting every experience he makes to suit his purpose.

Conclusion

Beginning with the philosophers of ancient Greece, we have seen how the individual is empowered to see himself at the centre of nature by placing value on himself. Rome adopted and preserved much of Greek culture, including the ideas of a rational natural order and natural law. Amid the turmoil of empire, however, a new concern arose for personal salvation, and the way was paved for the triumph of the Christian religion. Christian thinkers gradually found uses for their Greco-Roman heritage. The system of thought known as scholasticism, culminating in the work of Thomas Aquinas, resurrected reason as a tool of understanding but subordinated it to spiritual revelation and the revealed truths of Christianity. The intellectual and political edifice of Christianity, seemingly impregnable in the European Middle Ages, fell in turn to the assaults made on it by humanism, the Renaissance, and the Protestant Reformation. The Renaissance rediscovered much of classical culture and revived the notion of man as a creative being, while the Reformation, more directly but in the long run no less effectively, challenged the monolithic authority of the Roman Catholic Church. For Luther, as for Bacon or Descartes, and those who followed them, the way to truth or self-realization lies with the individual. From the above discussion, we see the individual evolving from a simple being who tried to understand nature and find answers to his problem by recourse to the forces of nature, to a complex being who now understands events of nature by the use of reason or by himself. He is rational and sensitive, emotional, active, confident and ready to venture. He has an aim and from the onset is endowed with the conviction that he can achieve the best possible. The individual, as we see today among others, is a rational being who possesses within himself the capacity for truth and goodness. He has dignity and has an enormous confidence in his power of reason as a source of profound understanding of human nature and of his place in the natural order. The average individual is, therefore, capable of taking responsibility for his own actions because he has the freedom to exercise his will.

CHAPTER 2

THE CONCEPT OF INDIVIDUALISM IN SOCIAL PHILOSOPHY

Introduction

The Western philosophical discussion of the individual, which sets out to make the individual more important than any other thing, as highlighted in the above chapter, has led to a dominance of individualism in the Western world. In this chapter, it will be made clear that this characterization is not far from right. "Like every ideology we shall see that contemporary individualism is partly a reaction against such constricting communities and practices, total subordination of individual interests under collective ones, which may lead to strict social control, wherein norms of the in-group are enforced on the person in need" (Jansz, 1991, p. 25). Individualism is associated with the liberty granted to the individual human being. This liberty seeks to offer its subjects the greatest degree of individual freedom. In line with this, in this chapter, we shall look at this offer to the individual in as far as society or state, economy and morality are concerned.

But we shall first try to understand what individualism is and what it is not.

Conceptual Definition of Individualism

According to *The Catholic Encyclopaedia* (2003*)*, a comprehensive and logical definition of individualism is not easy to obtain. However, it states that the definition given in the *Century Dictionary*, as *"That theory of government which favours non-interference of the State in the affairs of individuals"*, seems too narrow because it covers only one form of individualism, namely, political or civic individualism. It states that individualism is *"the tendency to magnify individual liberty, as against external authority, and individual activity, as against associated activity."* (The Catholic Encyclopaedia, 2003). One will understand external authority in this case to include not merely political and religious governments, but voluntary associations, and such forms of restraint as are found in general standards of conduct and belief. The Encyclopaedia Britannica (1994-2001, n. p.) sees individualism as *"that political and social philosophy that places high value on the freedom of the individual and generally stresses the **self-directed, self-contained**, and **comparatively unrestrained individual or ego**"* (Encyclopaedia Britannica, 1994-2001, n. p.). It explains that as a philosophy, "individualism involves a value system, a theory of human nature, a general attitude or temper, and belief in certain political, economic, social, and religious arrangements" (Encyclopaedia Britannica, 1994-2001, n. p.). The value system may be described in terms of the fact that all values are man-centred, that is, they are experienced by human beings. This presupposes that the individual is an end in himself and is of supreme value, society being only a means to individual ends. In another development it ascertains that "all individuals are in some sense morally equal, and this equality is best expressed by the proposition that no one should ever be treated solely as a means to the well-being of another person" (Encyclopaedia Britannica, 1994-2001, n p.). As a general attitude we are made to understand that, "individualism embraces a high valuation on self-reliance, on privacy, and on respect for other individuals" (Encyclopaedia Britannica, 1994-2001, n. p.). It seems to encourage "opposition to authority and to all manner of control over the individual, especially when they are exercised by the state" (Encyclopaedia Britannica, 1994-2001). Anticipating and valuing "progress", individualism "subscribes to the right of the individual to be different from, to compete with, and to get ahead of or fall behind others. Freedom of association extends to the right to join or refusal to join any organization." We are made to understand that only the most extreme individualist believe in anarchy, but the basic principle of the individualists is that government should keep its interference with human lives at a minimum and that it should confine itself largely to maintaining law and order, preventing individuals from interfering with others, and enforcing agreements (contracts) voluntarily arrived at. The state tends to be viewed as a necessary evil, and the slogan *"That government that governs least governs best"* is applauded (Leser, 1984, p.196).

Among others, individualism also implies a property system according to which each person enjoys the maximum of opportunity to acquire property and to manage and dispose of it as seen fit. The concept suggests that the interests of the normal adult are best served by allowing him maximum freedom and responsibility for choosing his objectives and the means for obtaining them, and acting accordingly. This belief follows from the conviction that each person is the best judge of his own interests and, granted equal opportunities, can discover how to advance them. This is further based on the assumption that this will contribute to the development of the individual and to the welfare of society, the latter because individualism is thought to provide the most effective incentive to productive endeavour.

Triandis (1995) confirms that the English political philosophers of the eighteenth and nineteenth centuries saw individualism as including ***ideas of maximum freedom of the individual***. He identified *authoritarianism* as the term that contrasted with individualism, denying the above-mentioned freedoms of the individual and requiring that individuals submit to the will of an authority, such as the king. He thinks that the term *collectivism* was a reaction that resulted from the eighteenth century individualistic ideas of the American Revolution (*all men are created equal, pursuit of happiness*) and the French Revolution (*liberty, equality, fraternity*).

Emergence of Individualism

Historians, philosophers and other scholars are not very sure about the originating 'point' of individualism. Some trace it back to classical Greece, among them, Leser (1984). He thinks that although individualism is a product of recent times, its roots are old. He states that in ancient there were philosophical forerunners like Kallikles and Zenon (Leser, 1984, p.196) .

This position is shared by many other scholars among them Triandis (1995) who also observed that the Greek sophists were individualist philosophers. The Greek sophists of the fifth century B.C. were among the first early individualist philosophers. For them the individual can decide how to behave without following the norms of one's in-group. Triandis (1995, p. 21) thinks that Plato and Socrates opposed the sophists because they did not have "*standards of what is good and proper.*" He believes that the word "***sophistry***" suggests that their reputation in the West has been poor. However, he argues further that the sophists' purpose was to teach their pupils to be successful in the courts, in debate, and in politics. Individual success is a key idea of individualism. The social organization of Athens, with its democracy, debates, and so on, made such skills valuable, and in fact the sophists were financially very successful.

The Encyclopaedia Britannica explains that although instances of individualism have occurred throughout history in many cultures and times, fully-fledged individualism, as it is usually conceived to be, seems to have emerged first in England, especially after the publication of the ideas of Adam Smith and Jeremy Bentham and their followers in economic and political theory. Smith's doctrine of laissez-faire, based upon a profound belief in the natural harmony of individual wills and Bentham's utilitarianism, with the basic rule of *"each to count for one and none for more than one,"* set the stage for these developments (Encyclopaedia Britannica, 1994-2001).

Triandis (1995) asserts that a major attempt to understand English individualism was made by Macfarlane (1978) who provided evidence that there was individualism in Britain as early as A.D. 1200. He paid much attention to the institution of primogeniture where the oldest son inherited the land so that property would not be divided. The other sons had to make their way as well as they could in society, and since they had learned about the good life, they struggled hard through various entrepreneurial activities to become rich. The presence of other resources as well as opportunities for commerce made affluence possible. Affluence leads to individualism. Also the system resulted in a good deal of immigration to the colonies, and immigrants tend to be more individualistic, since they leave their in-groups behind (Triandis, 1995, p. 21). Other thinkers link individualism quite strictly to private property. It is seen as having important disciplinary and judicial consequences, because the goods and their owner had to be protected. Private property provided the proprietor with a public, and thus visible, means to establish and express the difference between him and other people. His possessions contributed to his 'unicity,' and thus to an individualistic conception of man (Jansz, 1991, p. 26).

Still others think ecology also contributed a great deal to individualism. Triandis (1995) writes that from about the sixteenth century, the ecology of Western Europe began to be altered drastically with human beings exerting greater control over their ecology. He sees numerous factors contributing to this change. Among them are the rise of international trade, the rise of nation states, the formation of a merchant class, rapid development in science and technology, increased agricultural efficiency, industrialization, urbanization, and the rise of capitalism. These changes combine to create a radical shift from subsistence economies, which are largely determined by ecology to market economies, which are created by human intervention. The result is rapid social change, including much social strife. This led to the destruction of existing groups, making it necessary for individuals to act alone. Similarly, when there is much social mobility, individuals do not conform to groups. Others saw individualism as typical of hunting societies, where the immediate return from one's efforts and no possibility of food accumulation leads to equality. There is little property and authority, unfixed dwellings, and much geographical mobility, all of which lead to individualism. Schooler, (as cited in Triandis, 1995), reviewed the work of Macfarlane (1978) and pointed out that *individualism emerges when property rights are attached to individuals rather than to groups* (Triandis 1995, p. 21).

As already mentioned in chapter one, an important step towards modern individualism was taken in the *Humanism* of the Renaissance in fifteenth century Italy. This concerned itself with the dignity of the individual. It took shape in accord with a sense of personal autonomy that came to characterize humanism as a whole. It saw intelligence as capable of critical scrutiny and self-inquiry. Free intelligence and the intellectual virtue could analyze experience as an integral part of that more extensive virtue that could, according to many humanists, go far in conquering fortune. Backed by medieval sources but more sweeping and insistent in their approach, spokesmen such as Petrarch, Manetti, Valla, and Ficino asserted the individual's earthly pre-eminence and unique potentialities. Pico della Mirandola conveyed this notion with unprecedented vigour. Humanity, he asserted, had been assigned no fixed character or limit by God but instead was free to seek its own level and create his own future. No dignity, not even divinity itself, was forbidden to human aspiration (Encyclopaedia Britannica, 1994-2001).

Another important contributor worth mentioning is the rationalist philosopher René Descartes. His epistemological individualism asserts that the source of knowledge lies in the mind (*ratio*) of the individual. His 'Cogito ergo sum', implies a self-sufficient and competent one who is capable of living and conducting well-reasoned thought. Through introspection the individual is able to gain knowledge and control over his own mind, and consequently over the external world, his own body included.

Jansz (1991) thinks that the Renaissance individualism is quite different from its twentieth century counterpart in two respects. In the first place, Renaissance individualism was based on respect for talent or property and legal rights, but invariably stopped short of an interest in the drama of an idiosyncratic inner life. Furthermore, in the Renaissance, individualism was assumed and practiced almost exclusively among the male cultural elite. For him the embedding of the solitary individual in late nineteenth century society among others was the result of the industrial production. He observed that the last two centuries have given way to changes towards individualization in producing commodities and wealth that were unprecedented in history. This has led to a drastic reorganization of social life, which had far reaching consequences for individualization. Another one is schooling, linked of course, to production where people are educated to be productive. He observed that the institutionalized education of the child became centred upon its individualistic capacities. The third is the Reformation, which resulted in a new conception of the individual believer. This had an enormous impact on everyday thought and behaviour of the individual throughout Western history. People go to church and actively participate in the ritualized practices. The religious system of belief is thus put into direct practice, drawing the congregants into an explicit evaluation of their own thought and behaviour (Jansz, 1991, pp. 26-37)

What Individualism Is Not

Stata (1992, n. p.) points out that the first misconception of individualism is that it is taken to mean isolation or being alone and for that matter being outside society. For him the concept of individualism does not make sense in the absence of other human beings. He sees individualism and collectivism as contrasting views of the relationship between the individual and the group. He states that "***individualism is called 'individualism' not because it exhorts the individual to seek a life apart from others, but because it asserts that the individual, and not the group, is the most valuable in the society***" (Stata, 1992, n. p.). He goes on to explain that the belief that individualism means being alone leads people to say individualism is incompatible with cooperation. Usually, if one is too much of an 'individualist,' people say he cannot "get along with groups"; he is not a good "team player." Actually, a person who does not listen to others, the person who would rather do things in an inefficient way as long as it's "my way," is not being an "individualist," he's being closed minded. A true individualist wants the best for himself, so he seeks out the best, no matter who the source is. To the individualist, the truth is more important than any authority, including himself (Stata, 1992, n. p.). Tocqueville (n. d.) thinks that "*individualism is a novel expression, to which a novel idea has given birth.*" For him it does not mean selfishness, because selfishness is a passionate and exaggerated love of self, which leads a man to connect everything with himself and to prefer himself to everything in the world. Individualism is a mature and calm feeling, which disposes each member of the community to sever himself from the mass of his fellows and to draw apart with his family and his friends, so that after he has thus formed a little circle of his own, he willingly leaves society at large to itself. *Selfishness originates in blind instinct; selfishness blights the germ of all virtue; selfishness is a vice as old as the world, which does not belong to one form of society more than to another.*

Features of Individualism

Individualism focuses on the individual human being as the fundamental building block of society, or any other human group. The individual is the social world's 'ultimate constituent.' Consequently, society itself, which comes to existence only through a voluntary contract between individuals, is seen as nothing but a sum of these individuals. In this case, the individual has a primary reality, whereas society is a second order, derived or artificially constructed. Generally, this feature of individualism is connected with the second one which expresses individualism's view of morality. Here the dignity of the individual human being is central. Each person is viewed as an end in himself or herself and not as a means toward the fulfilment of the interests of someone else. Waterman (1981, p. 765) suggests the individual human being is the primary source of value, and collective goals are subsumed under personal ones. Another feature of individualism takes the individual human being and his or her social context as two distinct entities and assumes a clear distinction between these entities. Thus, Jansz (1991, p. 49) explains that "the individual is 'self-contained', meaning that he is delimited by 'firm boundaries that separate self from non self, marking each person as an independent event in the universe'. The individual is distinguished from his social and natural context; he is a *Homo Clausus* meaning closed man. There is a wall separating the individual and the society that surrounds him. He explains further that this wall that is visible is the skin.

Individualism assumes that all individuals are equal, at least in principle. The individual constituents of society should be granted equal respect. It also assumes that these equal individuals should be free from interference of others. They should also be free to develop their own life courses according to their personal plans, as individualistic cultures emphasized goals like self-sufficiency and self-glorification. Among individualists, power is desired and often achieved. The individualistic cultures had a view of the universe that included a struggle between individuals and gods. Triandis (1995) summarizes all these features, when he explains individualism versus collectivism in terms of ***achievement*** versus ***affiliation***, ***self-assertion*** versus ***respectfulness***, ***egalitarian*** versus ***hierarchical organization***, ***peer*** versus ***parental influences***, ***free*** versus ***constrained expression of ideas***, self-orientation versus other orientation, autonomy versus mutual dependence, fear of failure versus fear of rejection, principle centredness versus person centredness, organizational loyalty versus small group loyalty, encouragement of evaluation versus fear of evaluation, achieved versus ascribed criteria for promotion, fairness versus sacrifice, frankness versus not telling what one feels, self-importance versus self-effacement, being creative versus conforming, material versus spiritual, and valuing efficiency versus peace of mind. Individualism, according to Stata (1992, n. p.) holds that the individual is the unit of achievement. While not denying that one person can build on the achievements of others, individualism points out that achievement goes beyond what has already been done; it is something new that is created by the individual.

Individual and Civic Society

Society is characterized by such attributes as spontaneity, the self-contained social, economic, political, cultural and religious activity of its members, and their capacity to interact and cooperate. One of the essential dimensions of society is its political organization, embodied in the institution of a state. Usually, mutual relations connect society and the state. The state exerts an influence upon society through a network of governmental institutions, administrative, legislative, political, and ideological (Kuzmickas, n. d.).

When individualists assert that the individual is the primary unit of reality and the ultimate standard of value, they do not deny that societies exist or that people benefit from living in them. For them the society is essentially a summing up of individuals or a collection of individuals, not something over and above them. As pointed out above, living in society and cooperating with other people are tremendous benefits, which individualism does not deny. But individualism is skeptical that most arrangements of living and working with other men are not beneficial to the individual. Thus, individualism can be characterized concisely by its assumption that *the individual human being is the basic constituent of society* (Stata, 1992). Whiles thinkers like Aristotle and Hegel believed that societies developed naturally, others believe that individuals came together to form societies or states for various reasons. For the purpose of this work, we will look at the social contract theory which is more individual oriented.

The Social Contract Theory

Christman (2002) thinks that the tradition of thought that answers questions about the state with reference to individuals began in Europe in the seventeenth century, though its roots go further back than this. For him, prior to the sixteenth century, European thinkers understood the universe in an Aristotelian, teleological manner, where nature was thought to be organized according to an interlocking functional matrix whose operation contributed to an overall end, a *telos*. Royalty took their place not sanctioned from below by the consent of the governed, but by their superior place in the overall structure of humanity. States and kingdoms were evaluated according to how they flourished rather than whether they were 'just' in some modern sense.

As regards the social contract theorists themselves, the concept of natural right played an important role. The idea that individuals are endowed with certain innate rights to justifiably act according to their individual wills was indeed radical at the point when the social contract view was beginning to flourish. But through the overarching principles that specified the order of nature and dictated its proper functioning, natural law came to be seen in increasingly secular terms, as scientific laws rather than theological principles. Natural right also evolved from the specification of what is objectively right for an individual to do, to what subjectively an individual chooses to do. Conditions that resulted from free choice within the individual's natural rights, then, were seen as just, simply because such individuals rationally chose to produce those conditions. There was also the presumption that natural rights are exercised according to reason, in that the rights specified were those that allowed rational and moral action only. One did not have a natural right to act whimsically or in an evil manner. Putting these ideas together, then the relationship between the state and the individual came to be seen to rest on the choices people made within the dictates of reason and natural right. As we will see below, this combines two ideas that can in principle be separated: the idea that *the individual's choice justifies a state of affairs* and the idea that such a state is *justified because it is in the rational interest of the individual.*

Thomas Hobbes

Hobbes (1651) thinks that society is artificially created. By art, that great leviathan called a *commonwealth* or *state* (in Latin, *civitas*) is created. For him, the state is but an artificial man, though of greater stature and strength than the natural, for whose protection and defence it was intended; and in which the sovereignty is an artificial soul, as giving life and motion to the whole body; the magistrates and other officers of judicature and execution, artificial joints; reward and punishment (by which fastened to the seat of the sovereignty, every joint and member is moved to perform his duty) are the nerves, that do the same in the body natural; the wealth and riches of all the particular members are the strength; *salus populi* (*the people's safety*) its business; counsellors, by whom all things needful for it to know are suggested unto it, are the memory; equity and laws, an artificial reason and will; concord, health; sedition, sickness; and civil war, death. Lastly, the pacts and covenants, by which the parts of this body politic were at first made, set together, and united, resemble that fiat, or the let us make man, pronounced by God in the Creation (Hobbes, 1651).

Hobbes thinks that by nature the individual is a **selfish hedonist**. That is to say, *"of the voluntary acts of every man, the object is some good to himself"*. As human motives were, in their natural state, guided by unenlightened self-interest, these could, if left unchecked, have highly destructive consequences. Left unrestrained, humans, propelled by their internal dynamics, would crash against each other. He sees man as an egocentric individual who wants to maximize personal profit, and tries to minimize personal profit at the expense of other individuals. In seeking pleasure, individuals run into conflict with each other. In this "state of nature" i.e., before any civil state or rule of law, Hobbes thinks life would be "***solitary, poor, nasty, brutish*** and ***short***", leading to a "*war of every man against every man*". But he asserts that because all people are equal at least physically, possessing a passionate love of survival (***right of nature***) and some degree of rationality (***law of nature***), as life goes on, a viable, working society would arise as equilibrium between these competing forces. The logic is simple: any person's right of nature justifies violence against everybody else. Consequently, in the interests of personal survival, people will come around to agreeing that they should renounce their right to use violence.

Thomas Hobbes lived at a time when widespread warfare raged throughout Europe. The wars of religion in the sixteenth century and the Thirty Years' War in the seventeenth century are particularly bloody examples. He was also a witness to a great upheaval in English political life, where parliamentary armies rose up against and overthrew Charles I. The idea that life without a strong central authority would result in a 'war of all against all' was therefore not difficult for him to imagine.

As a mechanist and a materialist he believed that natural phenomena were made up only by physical elements that functioned according to deterministic laws of cause and effect. Human beings were no different, nor were their voluntary actions. For Hobbes, voluntary movement (what he called 'animal' motion) was caused by the external impact of some force on the senses proceeding to internal motions that are either helped (pleasure) or hindered (pain), issuing eventually (or not) in external movement. Such a system would operate according to a fundamental principle of continual motion, so that the most aversive eventually would be death (the ceasing of all motion). So, for Hobbes, the most fundamental drive for all human beings was self-preservation, a drive that necessarily out-ranked any other competing desire, such as the possible desire to advance another's welfare (Christman, 2002, p.28). Similarly, Hobbes is widely understood as the prototypical representative of *'psychological egoism.'* This egoism is the descriptive claim that as a matter of psychological fact, the fundamental motive for all human beings is self-interest. Although people may at times act to serve the interests of others or take others' concerns into account, their ultimate aim is to advance their own interests. In this case, they treat the satisfaction of others' needs as purely instrumental in the final accomplishment of their own goals. With this psychological picture before us, we can now see how Hobbes' vision of life outside of society was structured. Since all are completely selfish in the way described above, they will act in others' interests only as a result of social conventions, laws, social practices and rules of behaviour backed up by formal and informal sanctions. Without these sanctions, people would have no immediate motive not to wilfully pursue their own aims. Also, without established institutions (such as armies, police forces, and the like), all individuals would enjoy roughly the same level of power to accomplish their aims. No person or group of people could dominate others to accomplish their goal. It is obvious that given the inevitable conflicts of desires among individuals, there would be constant violence and danger, for all would do what they could to accomplish their own goals. Naturally, therefore, they will encounter others of equal power doing the same resulting in the famous '*war of every man against every man*' (Christman, 2002, p. 30).

That we may better understand this approach to political authority, two classical examples have been worked out by Christman (2002) to help us grasp the full nature of the problem of social coordination among self-interested individuals acting rationally, but separately, and without any pre-existing mechanism of enforcement or rules. In his story, if two people encounter each other in such a situation, they may face an interactive situation that game theorists have labelled a *Prisoner's Dilemma*. This well-studied problem involves a choice situation, where two independent actors must make a decision, which will affect their respective well-being. In very general terms, he explains that a *Prisoner's Dilemma* (PD) obtains when the two actors face a choice situation where they would both be better off if they chose one option together (cooperated) but individually advantaged if they did not do so (defected). If they both could be assured that their counterparts would cooperate, they would be made best off by cooperating, but short of having that assurance, it is better for each of them not to cooperate. Since each of them is made individually better off by choosing the non-cooperative option and without enforcement mechanisms in place to assure them that the other person will act cooperatively, they both choose the non-cooperative option, despite its being less advantageous than if they acted cooperatively together.

In clear terms, he pictures the prospect of a two person exchange without any way to enforce the agreement underlying the exchange, a nefarious exchange of money for contraband, where the only factors relevant to the choice of action is the outcome of the exchange as an example. The agreement is for one to leave a briefcase of money on a pre-assigned park bench, while another person simultaneously leaves the contraband at a park bench four blocks away. By the time you get to the other briefcase to find out if the contraband is in it, your counterpart might be looking at the case you left to see if you left the money in it. You supposedly will never see this person again and will suffer (you hope) no repercussion if you leave an empty case (the other person can hardly go running to the police).

Also, a parallel choice problem arises when a group decides to gather together to perform some joint task (the *'collective action problem'*). If there is no enforcement mechanism to induce compliance like suffering from a bad reputation or losing friends and the like, or experiencing the joy of commingling with friends for its own sake, it will be in everyone's individual interest to stay at home and let the others perform the task. For either enough people will show up and you will not be needed, in which case you waste your time and energy going out there, or they will not, in which case you really blow your day since you show up for nothing. Now you, like everyone else, would prefer the task to be accomplished. But since everyone acting individually and with self-interested motives reasons the same way you do, then everyone fails to show up (though interestingly enough, selfishness is not strictly necessary for this problem to arise). So again, although everyone acting together would prefer outcome A (the exchange made or the task getting done) to outcome B (no deal or no task), B results because everyone acts as an individual to maximize his or her own interests. So, as a group, everyone loses.

Now, looking at Hobbes in his state of nature, where all individuals are rationally self-interested in the way specified, the interactions among people take on the structure of a prisoner's dilemma (PD) and a collective action problem. For Hobbes, *there are no enforceable covenants or promises in the state of nature.* Morality, including rights and obligations, only holds power over people when there is some enforcement mechanism in place to give them reasons to conform to it. Without such things, morality does not exist.

Moreover, one can reasonably predict that many in the area (and even oneself on occasion) will be so moved by ambition, avarice, anger, and other passions that even if it were perfectly rational to cooperate, many will not. More so it will always be better to pre-emptively renege on a bargain than to be left holding the (empty) bag, while another breaks his or her promise and acts non-cooperatively. So he concludes that natural cooperation among people will not occur, even though the establishment of such cooperation would make it reasonable to continue to cooperate. Only when an external power is constructed, one to which all the rest of us hand over our individual abilities to exact our will (our weapons), will there exist a mechanism to enforce promises, contracts, laws, and indeed, all the rest of morality and public law. This is the beginning of civil society for Hobbes and the ground for its justification as well. Granting of complete sovereign power to one entity, while forsaking all of their individual abilities to act on selfish interests, establishes political authority and delivers them all from the state of nature, a state of endless war and conflict. Moreover, since the state of nature was so full of conflict and opposition, where no plans could be made, peaceful lifestyles pursued, property protected, or even survival assured, any civil society that ensures some measure of peace and survival will be in one's rational interest to enter. What we have just been saying is that individuals came together to form a society or a state for their own interest. According to Hobbes, sovereignty is established out of the voluntary, rational action of those governed. The sovereign, for Hobbes, stands in an 'agency' relation to the individual. That is, however he acts, unless he directly attacks the citizens and threatens their lives, he always acts in their interest. His power to protect the citizens from each other and from external enemy justifies his action. For this reason, Hobbes claimed that the sovereign could not ever injure the citizens by definition, for to injure someone is to act in a way contrary to their interests. The sovereign's existence and all its acts are effectively an extension of the citizens' individual wills, and since we cannot injure ourselves when we (rationally) decide to do something, he, as our agent, cannot injure us.

The initial attractiveness of granting political authority through a social contract stems from the assumption that individuals are legitimately bound only by an authority that they have, in some sense, chosen for themselves. Like all other voluntary actions, the decision to live under the authority of a political regime is an extension of our own free will; so the authority we live under is simply a case of obeying ourselves. As we have seen, Hobbes is an individualist in his analysis and evaluation of social phenomenon (Hampton, 1986; Macpherson, 1962). That is to say, the claims he makes about societies take as the fundamental unit of analysis the individual person, a person described with characteristics that never necessarily include her or his relation to others. While such individuals may well be members of families, be part of a religious tradition that defines their values, understand themselves as fundamentally moulded by tradition, or the like, none of that is directly relevant to understanding what is rational for them to do (Christman, 2002, p. 30).

John Locke

While Hobbes, in his *Leviathan* (1651), asserts that, the state of nature was one in which there were no enforceable criteria of right and wrong, a situation in which each person took for himself all that he could, resulting in life being "solitary, poor, nasty, brutish and short" and in a state of war, which could be ended only if individuals agreed (in a social contract) to give their liberty into the hands of a sovereign, who was thenceforward absolute, on the sole condition that their lives were safeguarded by sovereign power, Locke (in the second of *Two Treatises of Government*, 1690) thinks that in the state of nature the rights of life and property were generally recognized under natural law, the inconveniences of the situation arises from insecurity in the enforcement of those rights (Christman, 2002, p. 48).

Locke begins his argument with a picture of the state in which man is naturally in the state of perfect freedom and equality, wherein all power and jurisdiction is reciprocal. This refers, of course, to the state of nature. The basis of Locke's theory is that, independent of social conventions and civil obligations, all human beings have certain natural moral rights that all other human beings know by reason and they are obliged to respect. This means that the state of nature for Locke is a very different place from the chamber of horrors described by Hobbes. Despite our natural freedom, we have no right to destroy ourselves and we have no right to harm others. Indeed, we have an obligation *'to preserve the rest of Mankind'*, when doing so does not threaten our own lives, a view quite at odds with the Hobbesian right of all to all things. Further, we have no right to violate others' natural rights to life, liberty, and possessions. This conception of people's natural understanding of morality indicates why, eventually, all people would want to move into civil society. For just as every person has rights to health, liberty, and possessions, so has everyone also a right to enforce the protection of those rights by way of punishing violators. Indeed, someone whose natural capacities do not prevent him from either understanding or following the moral law is like a '*Wild Savage Beast*' and may be destroyed as a Lion or a Tiger. Since individuals are not always precise in their estimations of the amount of punishment deserved for particular transgressions and because those accused of crimes will often react violently against such punishments, such a spiral of conflict will make continued life in the state of nature inconvenient. There will be lack of any superior common judge with the authority to settle disputes such as this. People will naturally come together to create an institution that will function as such a judge. This means that although by nature we all have certain rights and duties, we cannot effectively enjoy such rights securely unless we live under a common political authority. This, then, is the motive for civil society for Locke. The authority created in such a society, then, is based solely on the consent of those governed. We should note, though, that the assumption that even without a centralized political authority people nevertheless are obliged by various rights and duties in Locke's view, obviates the problem which plagued Hobbes' picture, namely how those not subject to promissory obligations can make a promise to create a centralized authority to enforce promises. For Locke, individuals are bound by their promises and agreements in the state of nature by virtue of the natural rights we all enjoy and which we all recognize through reason, even where there is no enforcement mechanism to support anyone's claim of a breach.

When people in Locke's state of nature are imagined to congregate to create a civil society, two separate acts of agreement take place. The first is the initial decision to gather as a society at all, and this agreement must be unanimous to be binding on all participants; anyone dissenting from such an agreement simply remains in the state of nature relative to the others. However, subsequent to this initial social formation, another agreement, namely an agreement to form a particular governmental structure, is made. This agreement need not be unanimous for Locke, but can proceed simply by majority rule. These original contracts, then, create civil society and put in place the centralized political authority of the state, with whatever legislative and executive apparatus chosen by the contractees.

The natural rights one exercises in consenting to adhere to a political authority fix the grounds for the legitimacy of that authority. For this reason, Locke argues that rebellion is justified whenever a sovereign acts in ways that are in violation of individuals' natural rights. Arbitrary or absolute power on the part of the sovereign is never justified and is automatically grounds for resistance and rebellion. Any sovereign act, which runs counter to the protection of the natural rights of the governed, automatically nullifies the legitimate authority of that sovereign. Recent followers of John Locke argue that the existence of state power is at best a necessary evil and, in order to be consistent with our natural rights must be confined only to the functions of protecting people against overt harm. Political obligation, in this view, rests on the degree to which such states succeed in protecting these pre-political prerogatives that all human beings enjoy independent of the existence of any government. For Lockean libertarians, most notably, such rights include the right to private property. States are therefore legitimate only if they protect the rights of property owners from incursions of such rights, including unapproved governmental regulation, taxation, or the like. What is distinctive of contemporary Lockeans in general, however, is the view that legitimate state authority rests on the consent of the governed, where such consent expresses the natural rights they all enjoy independent of the existence of the state (The Catholic Encyclopedia, 2003).

Jean-Jacques Rousseau

In another development, the social contract theory of Jean-Jacques Rousseau (1775) also explains that society or the State was merely the outcome of a compact freely made by its individual citizens. To keep society going with peace and confidence, an artifice must be worked into the social contract. Accordingly, the State was merely the outcome of a compact freely made by its individual citizens. Consequently they were under no moral obligation to form a State, and the State itself was not a moral necessity (Audi, 1999, p. 800). Rousseau, as a social contract theorist, attempts to construct a hypothetical state of nature to explain the current human situation. Rousseau (1775) presents us with an almost idyllic view of humanity. In nature humans are first seen as little more than animals except for their special species, sympathy. Later, through an explanation of the development of reason and language, humans, while retaining their sympathetic quality, were able to understand their individual selves. This leads to natural community and the closest thing to what Rousseau considers humanity's perfect moment. He thinks that private property, which quickly followed division of labour, was responsible for human's alienation from one another. Thus, we see man who '*was born in freedom, now finding himself in chains*' (Audi, 1999, p. 800). With an account of the practical role of the legislator and the introduction of the concept of the *General Will*, Rousseau attempts to give us a foundation for good government by presenting a solution to the conflicts between the particular and the universal, the individual and the citizen, and actual and the moral. Individuals, freely agreeing to a social pact and giving up their rights to the community, are assured of the liberties and equality of political citizenship found in the contract. It is only through being a citizen that the individual can fully realize his freedom and exercise his moral rights and duties. While the individual is naturally good, he must always guard against being dominated or dominating.

Rousseau finds a solution to the problems of individual freedoms and interests in a superior form of moral/political action that he calls the general will. The individual, as citizen, substitutes *'I must'* for *'I will'* which is also an *'I shall'* when it expresses assent to the general will. The general will is a universal force or statement more noble than any particular will. In willing his own interest, the citizen is at the same time willing what is communally good. The particular and the universal are united. The individual human participant realizes himself in realizing the good of all.

As a practical political commentator, Rousseau knew that the universal and the particular do not always coincide. For this reason he introduced the idea of the legislator, which allows the individual citizen to realize his fulfilment as social being and to exercise his individual rights through universal consent. In moments of difference between the majority will and the general will, the legislator will instil the correct moral/political understanding. This will be represented in the laws. While sovereignty rests with the citizens, Rousseau does not require that political action be direct.

Rousseau (1762), argued that only when society is arranged so that individuals can participate directly in the development of legislation can a type of sovereignty be established, where a person obeys only himself and remains free. The type of freedom Rousseau had in mind in these arguments was a type of 'positive' freedom, where to be free means to be self-governing. He goes on to explain that since others in one's society also have interests and needs that they will insist upon satisfying, one retains one's freedom in this sense only when one interacts with those individuals in finding a solution to such conflicts of interest. This solution, he believes, will be expressed in a collective decision of the 'general will.' The individual citizen, then, must submit completely to the general will, since that expression of collective interest is the best balance of competing interests that collective interaction in the society can produce. Therefore, to be individually self-governing, for Rousseau, is to participate (and have one's interests reflected) in collective self-government (Encyclopaedia Britannica, 1994-2001). Rousseau held that *in the state of nature man was unwarlike and somewhat undeveloped in his reasoning powers and sense of morality and responsibility*. When, however, people agreed for mutual protection to surrender individual freedom of action and establish laws and government, they acquired a sense of moral and civic obligation. In order to retain its essentially moral character, government must thus rest on the consent of the governed, the *volonté générale* (*"general will"*) (Encyclopaedia Britannica, 1994-2001). While Hobbes bases political legitimacy on its consistency with rationality and Locke on its consistency with natural rights, Rousseau bases such legitimacy on the demands of freedom. With Hobbes, we saw that no act of will was necessary for the legitimating of the state, but the movement from the state of nature to a civil society must have been one that was consistent with the rational interests of those making such a move. With Locke, actual expressions of consent, even if tacitly expressed through indirect means, were necessary for political justification. A shift occurs with Rousseau, who still maintains a focus on the will as the source of legitimacy, but no longer requires that outward acts of consent to the beginnings of a civil society be in evidence.

What we have tried to do as regards the individual and society is the examination of the social contract view of Thomas Hobbes, bringing out his basic commitment to an egoistic conception of human beings. We have also seen a justification of the authority of the state based on the rational self-interest of those governed by it. Apparently, that is against the backdrop of a state of nature that was barely tolerable for those in it. Hobbes argued for the authority of an all-powerful sovereigns based on the rational interest of the governed. We noted that his justification was not based on the actual wills of the governed but rather on their rational interests. Locke's version of the social contract, exhibits a 'will' theory of political authority, and rests on a view of human nature (and the state of nature) that considers all human beings to be capable of recognizing their own and others' natural rights. With Rousseau, political authorities are no longer justified with reference to their origins; rather the fundamental role of political institutions in establishing citizens' freedom becomes central (Locke, n. d.).

As far as the society or the state is concerned, individualism sees an agreement between the ruled and their rulers, defining the rights and duties of each. This, as has been seen above, is based on the theory that, individuals were born into an anarchic state of nature, which was happy or unhappy according to the particular version. They then, by exercising natural reason, formed a society (and a government) by means of a contract among themselves. The important point is that the State will be given a monopoly on violence and absolute authority. In return, the State promises to exercise its absolute power to maintain a state of peace. Consequently, government should confine itself largely to maintaining law and order, preventing individuals from interfering with others, and enforcing agreements (contracts) voluntarily arrived at.

The Individual and Economy

As we have seen above, under individualism, the individual is sovereign. He, whose cooperation is to be obtained only through voluntary agreement, is an end in himself. All people are seen acting as traders, either voluntarily agreeing to interact or going separate ways; for them, it's either "win-win, or no deal." The government is limited strictly to ensuring that coercion is banished from human relations, that 'voluntary' is really voluntary, that both sides choose freely to deal and both sides live up to their agreements. "The individual, called a market man by Locke, is motivated by self-interest. He will enter a relation only because of his own interest". (Locke, n. d.).

According to the laissez-faire school of economists and politicians, the State should permit and encourage the fullest freedom of contract and of competition throughout the field of industry. This theory, which was derived partly from the political philosophy of the eighteenth century, as already mentioned, and partly from the Kantian doctrine that stipulates the individual has a right to the fullest measure of freedom that is compatible with the equal freedom of other individuals, and partly from the teachings of Adam Smith, received its most systematic expression in the tenets of the Manchester School. Its advocates opposed not only such public enterprises as state railways and telegraphs, but such restrictive measures as factory regulations, and laws governing the hours of labour for women (Encyclopaedia Britannica, 1994-2001).

Smith's (Encyclopaedia Britannica, 1994-2001) "obvious and simple system of natural liberty" pictured exchange of goods and services in free and competitive markets as the ideal system of cooperation for mutual advantage. Such an organization should maximize efficiency as well as freedom, secure for each participant the largest yield from his resources to be had without injury to others, and achieve a just distribution, meaning a sharing of the social product in proportion to individual contributions. Capitalism is looked upon as the political system compatible with individualism. By capitalism we mean a system based on the recognition of individual rights, including property rights, in which all property is privately owned. A system where any or all forms of government intervention in production and trade is abolished, and State and Economics are separated in the same way and for the same reasons as the separation of Church and State (Encyclopaedia Britannica, 1994-2001). As mentioned earlier, it is a system based on the notion that individuals are traders, either voluntarily agreeing to interact or going separate ways, a system in which government is limited strictly to ensuring that coercion is banished from human relations, that 'voluntary' is really voluntary, that both sides choose freely to deal.

Also called Free Market Economy, or Free Enterprise Economy, it is seen as the economic system, dominant in the Western world since the breakup of feudalism, in which most of the means of production are privately owned and production is guided and income distributed largely through the operation of markets. (Encyclopaedia Britannica, 1994-2001)

What distinguished capitalism from previous systems was the use of the excess of production over consumption to enlarge productive capacity rather than to invest in economically unproductive enterprises such as pyramids and cathedrals. This characteristic was encouraged by several historical events. In the ethic encouraged by the Protestant Reformation of the 16th century, traditional disdain for acquisitive effort was diminished, while hard work and frugality were given a stronger religious sanction. Economic inequality was justified on the grounds that the wealthy were also the virtuous. In his book *The Protestant Ethic and the Spirit of Capitalism* (1904-5), Weber argued *'Protestant ethic'* — the famous *'work ethic'* — the drive for economic success, the will to work hard, the habit of not spending on frivolous self-indulgence — all this, originating in theology, provided a 'spirit' for capitalism the set of motivations and attitudes that led to 'rational investment' of profits. The ideology of classical capitalism was expressed in Adam Smith's *Inquiry into the Nature and Causes of the Wealth of Nations*

(1776), which recommended leaving economic decisions to the free play of self-regulating market forces. After the French Revolution and the Napoleonic Wars had swept the remnants of feudalism into oblivion, Smith's policies were increasingly put into practice. The performance of capitalism since World War II in the United States, the United Kingdom, Germany, Austria, France, and Japan, to mention but a few, has given evidence of its continued vitality.

For example, with few exceptions, the production and distribution of all goods and services were entrusted to market forces rather than to the rules and regulations that had abounded a century earlier. The level of wages was likewise mainly determined by the interplay of the supply of and the demand for labour, not by the rulings of local magistrates. Profits were exposed to competition rather than protected by government monopoly. Perhaps of greater importance in perceiving Smith's world as capitalist, as well as market-oriented, is its clear division of society into an economic and a political realm. The role of government had been gradually narrowed until Smith could describe its duties as consisting of only three functions: (1) the provision of national defence, (2) the protection of each member of society from the injustice or oppression of any other, and (3) the erection and maintenance of those public works and public institutions (including education) that would not repay the expense of any private enterpriser, although they might "do much more than repay it" to society as a whole. The result is if the realm of government had been greatly delimited, that of commerce had been greatly expanded (Encyclopaedia Britannica, 1994-2001).

Based on the above idea on sovereignty of the market and the "natural harmony of interests" it is argued that if individuals are left free to pursue their self-interest in an exchange economy based upon a division of labour, the welfare of the group as a whole will necessarily be enhanced. The one propelling force is the selfishness of the individual, which becomes harnessed to the public good. This is because in an exchange economy the individual must serve others in order to serve himself. It is only in a free market, however, that this happy consequence can ensue. Any other arrangement will lead to regimentation, exploitation, and economic stagnation. Furthermore, it is observed that unlike controlled economy, where progress is directed by a planning agency acting at the behest of the government, in the individualist economy, this is accomplished in the free market through the price mechanism. In such a market system the theoretically free choices of individual buyers and sellers determine how the resources of society (labour, goods, capital) shall be employed. These choices manifest themselves in bids and offers that in their totality determine the price at which a commodity will sell. Theoretically, when the demand for a commodity is great, prices will rise, making it profitable for producers to increase the supply; as supply approximates demand, prices will tend to fall until producers divert productive resources to other uses. In this way the closest possible coincidence is said to be achieved between what is wanted and what is produced. The system is asserted to assure a reward in proportion to merit. The assumption is that in a freely competitive economy in which no one is barred by status from engaging in economic activity, the income received from such activity is a fair measure of its value to society. Individuals, therefore, determine through the prices they pay and through the amount of their purchases both the quantity and quality of production. They determine directly the prices of consumers' goods, and thereby indirectly the price of all material factors of production and the wages of all hands employed. The individual consumers are the masters, to whose whims the entrepreneurs and capitalists must adjust their investments and methods of production. The individual chooses the entrepreneurs and the capitalists and removes them as soon as they prove failures. Presupposed in the foregoing analyses is a conception of the individual as an economic animal rationally engaged in minimizing costs and maximizing gains (wages, profit, interest). Egoistic and hedonistic assumptions about human nature, which were taken for granted, led easily to an emphasis on man as a forward-looking and end-seeking creature. "*When matters of such importance as pain and pleasure is at stake . . . who is there that does not calculate?*" Bentham asked. To prove his case, Bentham assumes that even would-be lawbreakers carefully balance the pleasure to be derived from their contemplated crime against the pain of punishment, it could be affirmed that they would also meticulously balance utilities against costs at the marketplace. Since rational men best know their own interest, it must follow that interference by agencies of government could only diminish that "greatest happiness of the greatest number" that the followers of Bentham claimed to desire (*The Catholic Encyclopedia*, 2003).

Implied by the logic of this economic creed is a functional justification of private property, often buttressed, to be sure, by a doctrine of natural right to shield manifestly functionless claims to property. John Locke's *Two Treatises of Government* (1690) pointed the way by defining property as "whatsoever . . . [man] hath mixed his labour with. . . ." Adam Smith asserts that "the property which every man has in his own labour . . . is the original foundation of all property. . . ." And Bentham noted that "it is this right that has overcome the natural aversion to labour. . . ." Since acquisitiveness and indolence were regarded as inborn and ineradicable human traits, security of property had to be preserved if incentive was not to be destroyed and the production of goods discouraged. Both French revolutionaries and English gentry could be rallied to such a defence of property; and the *American Constitution* as well as the *French Declaration of the Rights of Man and of the Citizen*, both of them liberal testaments, charge government with basic responsibility for its protection (Jansz,1991, pp. 26-37).

Under capitalism, therefore, the government protects rights, including the right to property. Without the right to use and dispose what one has produced, one has no liberty. If individuals cannot work and produce towards goals, they cannot pursue happiness. If one cannot consume the product of one's effort, one cannot live. If a government does not protect property rights, an individual is a slave at the mercy of someone or some group.

The Individual and Morality

There is a sense in which all men are ethical individualists, that is, inasmuch as they hold the voice of conscience to be the immediate rule of conduct. But ethical individualism means more than this. It means that the individual conscience, or the individual reason, is not merely the decisive subjective rule, but that it is the only rule. It assumes that there is no objective authority or standard, which it is bound to take into account. Among the most important forms of the theory is *intuitionism* or common sense morality of the Scottish School to which Hutchinson, Reid, Ferguson, and Smith belonged, the autonomous morality of Kant and all those systems of Hedonism which make individual value or pleasure the supreme criterion of right and wrong (Christman, 2002, p. 42). In line with the above, individualists will see religious beliefs and salvation as personal. As we have noted above, the reformation resulted in a new conception of the individual believer. People went to church and actively participated in the ritualized practices as individuals. The religious system of belief is thus put into direct practice, drawing the faithful into an explicit evaluation of their own thought and behaviour (Christman, 2002, pp. 43-48)

This resulted in self-responsible individuals acting, not so much in terms of laws from the outside, but in terms of a developing realization of self-worth and respect for the other. Like other thinkers in this tradition, Hobbes also specifies the Natural Laws that apply to human behaviour. The general definition of a law of nature for human beings, says Hobbes, is that of a general rule 'found out by Reason, by which a man is forbidden to do that, which is destructive for his life. The first, fundamental law of nature, then, is to seek peace, and when that is not possible, to do whatever is necessary to defend oneself. In a state of nature (a war of all against all), it follows that everyone has a 'right' to everything, 'even to one another's body,' when that is necessary for survival. But the second fundamental law of nature, for Hobbes, is that a person should be willing, when others are also, to lay down his right to invade his neighbour's possessions in so far as peace and security can be established as a result. Hobbes then lists seventeen further laws of nature, such as keeping one's covenants, returning good will to those who benefit you, cooperating with others, pardoning offences, and the like.

In his *Letter Concerning Toleration,* Locke argues that external coercion for the purpose of inducing religious faith is not so much morally abhorrent as it is ineffective, and so, in a sense, absurd. For, to have faith is to grasp internally, for one's own reasons, the truth of the theological doctrine, which is being apprehended (as well as the moral obligations that arise from it). For Locke no external force can induce a person to understand the truth of such doctrines, for if that were attempted, the person would be assenting to the doctrine for reasons of expediency (avoiding the punishment threatened for example) rather than its truth (Christman, 2002, p. 95). We can conclude therefore that to validly bind individuals, moral obligations must be apprehended by the person bound by them 'from the inside', as it were, rather than imposed on him by an external force. For the individualist, all individuals have the right that others do not harm them in their enjoyment of good things of life. Rights and the obligations are seen as correlative, and being both universal and "negative" in character, are capable under normal circumstances of being enjoyed by all simultaneously. It is the universality of the human right not to be killed, injured, or robbed. In his *Second Treatise* Locke states boldly that, *because we are God's handiwork (and He would not have created us unless we had the capacity to follow norms that are necessary for our survival), we all have a natural capacity for Reason, which gives us direct access to the moral law which Locke classified as the laws of nature.* As pointed out above, independent of social conventions and civil obligations, all human beings have certain natural moral rights that all other human beings are obliged to respect because they know by reason. Natural freedom does not mean doing what one likes but doing what is right. Consequently, we have no right to destroy ourselves and we have no right to harm others. On the other hand we have the responsibility to preserve the rest of Mankind. Further, we have no right to violate others' natural rights to life, liberty, and possessions and so someone whose natural capacities prevent him from either understanding or following the moral law must be eliminated (Christman, 2002, pp. 96-97). In the arena of normative philosophy, Kant (1785) is best known as the source of '*deontological*' or *duty based moral theory*, an approach to moral reasoning that demands that rational agents consider the generalization of their proposed action when judging its moral acceptability. This procedure is one expression of Kant's *Categorical imperative*, with its dictates to universalize our maxims for action, never use another as merely a means to our ends, and to act as if we were legislators in a kingdom of ends. One way to put the basic principle of individualism then, is the claim for the equal moral status of all persons conceived as autonomous beings, who rationally and autonomously pursue things they judge to be worthwhile. Justice is formulated in a way that expresses this respect, where people are considered ultimately able to reflect upon and embrace (or reject or revise) conceptions of value for themselves. Thus, the overall approach to social justice that individualism embodies can be seen to rest on the ultimate valuation of persons as having a basic interest in pursuing their own conceptions of what is valuable.

This philosophy is committed to the protection of interests at the individual level, the person's interest in leading an autonomous life however that is conceptualized. That is not to say that the individualist insists that people should lead lives separated from history, commitments, traditions, and communities, but only that their interest in either embracing or, if they wish, rejecting such ways is of fundamental importance.

Since justice for them amounts to the protection of people's abilities to lead autonomous lives, the considerations of securing the rules of justice, the right, is of more basic importance than promoting any specific conception of what is valuable for people, the good. Only if people's abilities to pursue the good by their own lights and their autonomy protected by the rule of justice can the state concern itself with the promotion of people's good. Never can it do so in violation of that basic respect for autonomy. The rules of justice, the prohibitions and permissions that regulate social interaction are to be 'secured' and 'protected,' while the good, what is valuable, fulfilling, virtuous and worthwhile in human life is something that must be promoted. The liberal view being stated here is that such moral factors can be conceptually separated and securing the first is more basic than promoting the second.

What is distinctive is merely the particular conception of what makes a good life. It is seen as that life which is in pursuit of valuable ends endorsed by the person pursuing them from the inside. In our terminology, this amounts to claiming that the state should promote the good of its citizens by promoting their ability to live autonomous lives in pursuit of (what they take to be) objective values.

This issue could be seen as merely terminological, in that, the claim that equality of moral status is fundamental to liberalism is equivalent to stating that promoting (equally) the ability of citizens to live good lives is fundamental. The state should respect the equal status of persons in their pursuit of the good. This is different from claiming that the state should promote that good. The first insists that social relations among people (who are pursuing their own values) is the primary focus of justice and not the content of the lives those people lead.

The state is, therefore, seen in its purest form as anti-paternalistic and anti-perfectionist. It is anti-paternalistic in that it does not interfere with a rational autonomous person's pursuit of what he thinks good (for him) even if such interference is thought to promote the person's good from a more objective point of view. Its anti-perfectionism is merely a generalization of this stance in that the state does not promote the overall good for its citizens in a way that violates respect for the autonomous lives of those citizens. In another development, Tocqueville (n. d.) discusses how the Americans combat individualism by the principle of self-interest rightly understood. He explains that when the world was managed by a few rich and powerful individuals, these persons loved to entertain a lofty idea of the duties of man. They were fond of professing that it is praiseworthy to forget oneself and that good should be done without hope of reward, as it is by the Deity himself. Such were the standard opinions of that time in morals. He does not seem to believe that men were more virtuous in aristocratic ages than in others, but they were incessantly talking of the beauties of virtue, and its utility was only studied in secret. But since the imagination takes less lofty flights, and every man's thoughts are centred in himself, moralists are alarmed by this idea of self-sacrifice and they no longer venture to present it to the human mind.

For Tocqueville (n. d.), moralists content themselves with inquiring whether the personal advantage of each member of the community does not consist in working for the good of all; and when they have hit upon some point on which private interest and public interest meet and amalgamate, they are eager to bring it into notice. Observations of this kind are gradually multiplied; what was only a single remark becomes a general principle, and it is held as a truth that man serves himself in serving his fellow creatures and that his private interest is to do good. American moralists do not profess that men ought to sacrifice themselves for their fellow creatures because it is noble to make such sacrifices, but they boldly aver that such sacrifices are as necessary to him who imposes them upon himself as to him for whose sake they are made. This is because the Americans have found out that, in their country and their age, man is brought home to himself by an irresistible force; and, losing all hope of stopping that force, they turn all their thoughts to the direction of it. They therefore do not deny that every man may follow his own interest, but they endeavour to prove that it is the interest of every man to be virtuous.

This principle of self-interest rightly understood is not a lofty one but he sees it as clear and sure. It does not aim at mighty objects, but it attains without excessive exertion all those at which it aims. As it lies within the reach of all capacities, everyone can without difficulty learn and retain it. He asserts that the principle of self-interest rightly understood appears to him the best suited of all philosophical theories to the wants of the men of our time, and that he regards it as their chief remaining security against themselves. He suggests that the minds of the moralists of our age should turn towards it even if they should judge it to be incomplete; it must nevertheless be adopted as necessary. No power on earth can prevent the increasing equality of conditions from inclining the human mind to seek out what is useful or from leading every member of the community to be wrapped up in himself. It must therefore be expected that personal interest will become more than ever the principal if not the sole spring of men's actions; but it remains to be seen how each man will understand his personal interest. (Tocqueville, n.d)

Scheler (1913) shows that what one "ought to do" presupposes a feeling of the value of what ought to be done which is given a priori and which is anchored in each person's *ordo amoris*, an *"order, or logic, of the heart"* that is not congruent with the logic of reason. According to this logic, moral acts and deeds are individual and originate in an individual's pre-rational preferring (or rejecting) of values.

Observation

Even though critics have attributed loneliness, frustration, insecurity, selfishness, broken homes, unhealthy competition, depression and many other problems of modern man to individualism, one is always impressed at how the dignity and value of the individual is generally acknowledged in contemporary Western societies because of this concept. This is seen in their day-to-day activities. As pointed out above, across all sections of society the individual is accepted as such and well provided for. The draft constitution of the *European Union* testifies to this. Already in the preamble a clear sign of the importance or value of the individual is displayed when the fathers and mothers of the constitution expressed their consciousness that Europe is a continent that has brought forth civilisation and has gradually developed the values underlying humanism: equality of persons, freedom and respect for reason. They identify their inspiration as coming from the cultural, religious and humanist inheritance of Europe. They see this value as still present in its heritage. This has embedded within the life of society the central role of the human person and his or her inviolable and inalienable rights, and respect for law. They believe that when Europe is reunited in its diversity and continues along the path of civilisation, which gives ultimate value to the individual, human hope, progress and prosperity, for the good of all its inhabitants, including the weakest and most deprived will be realised. It is no wonder therefore that Article II concerns itself with the individual by making it clear that human dignity is inviolable and so must be respected and protected. Everyone has the right to life. Consequently it states categorically that *"No one shall be condemned to the death penalty, or executed"*. To safeguard the above, it stated that no one shall be subjected to torture or to inhuman or degrading treatment or punishment let alone be killed. No one shall be required to perform forced or compulsory labour let alone be owned as a property.

The constitution clearly shows its resentment to discrimination of all kinds. Any discrimination based on any ground such as sex, race, colour, ethnic or social origin, genetic features, language, religion or belief, political or any other opinion, membership of a national minority, property, birth, disability, age or sexual orientation shall be prohibited. It denounced distinction between men and women and states that equality between men and women must be ensured in all areas, including employment, work and pay. In order that children may grow to be responsible individuals the constitution makes it clear that children shall have the right to such protection and care as is necessary for their well-being. They may express their views freely. Such views shall be taken into consideration on matters, which concern them in accordance with their age and maturity. In all actions relating to children, whether taken by public authorities or private institutions, the child's best interests must be a primary consideration. Every child shall have the right to maintain on a regular basis a personal relationship and direct contact with the parents, unless that is contrary to his or her interests. Placing a ban on the employment of children, it pegged the minimum age of admission to employment at the school leaving age. When employed, young people should have working conditions appropriate to their age and be protected against economic exploitation and any work likely to harm their safety, health or physical, mental, moral or social development or to interfere with their education. In his old age the individual right to lead a life of dignity and in independence and to participate in social and cultural life is ensured. Persons with disabilities are not left out. The Union recognises and respects the right of persons with disabilities to benefit from measures designed to ensure their independence, social and occupational integration and participation in the life of the community. Furthermore, the individual is endowed with certain rights and freedoms that in no small way acknowledge the individual's wellbeing as primary to all. It ensures that everyone has the right to liberty and security of person. The individual's right of access to data, which has been collected concerning him or her, and the right to have it, rectified is provided for. The individual has the right to own, use, dispose of and bequeath his or her lawfully acquired possessions. The right to freedom of thought, conscience and religion is also acknowledged. Everyone has the right to freedom of expression. This right shall include freedom to hold opinions and to receive and impart information and ideas without interference by public authority and regardless of frontiers. Everyone has the right to freedom of peaceful assembly and to freedom of association at all levels, in particular in political, trade union and civic matters, which implies the right of everyone to form and to join trade unions for the protection of his or her interests.

Conclusion

That Western culture is highly individualistic is a fact that can hardly be denied. The public resources provided by the ideology of individualism are dominant in no small way. Western social life, public as well as private, has been pervaded by individualism. The opposition from the ideology of collectivism is not seen as strong. Individualism declares that in this society man is the supreme value; that human life is most precious; that the ultimate end of all social and state efforts is the creation of social conditions which enable everyone to become a well-rounded, developed personality, and that the higher standard of development of one person serves as a precondition for the higher development of others. So well is the individual provided for in the Western culture that even when he is found outside the culture, the draft European constitution provided for the fact that the individual shall, in the territory of a third country in which the Member State of which he or she is a national is not represented, be entitled to protection by the diplomatic or consular authorities of any Member State, on the same conditions as the nationals of that Member State.

CHAPTER THREE

THE TRIBAL SYSTEM IN GHANA AND THE INDIVIDUAL

Introduction

Having considered the concept of the individual in Western philosophy in the previous chapters with no intention to attempt to compare, we shall now look at the Ghanaian traditional concept of the individual bearing in mind that differences of details may exist from one traditional area to the other. But as Wiredu (1992, p.9) puts it, since *"a volume on Ghanaian philosophy is a volume in African philosophy"* we may say that although there are differences of detail and possibly in some cases, of principle in concepts, there exist deep affinities of both thought and feeling across the entirety of ethnic Africa. We shall then look at the place of the individual in the community. In other words, we shall look at the social, economic, and political organization of the traditional society and the individual. The chapter will end with a short look at morality and the individual in the traditional society.

Ghanaian Traditional Concept of the Individual

Ghana was formerly a British colony known as the Gold Coast, and was the first black nation in sub-Saharan Africa to achieve independence in 1957. One can identify approximately 100 ethno linguistic groups all further subdivided into numerous cultural and linguistic units (*Report on Ghana, 1994*), each conscious of its identity. The country is divided into sixteen regions almost on tribal basis. Apart from a few scholars who try to explain the concept of man in writing in the Akan tradition very little literature exists about the other tribes in Ghana on this topic. Even in his *African Religions and Philosophy*, Mbiti (*World Fact Book*, n. d.), writing about the origin of man mentioned the thoughts of some African tribes including the Asante, who are Akan speaking and the Ewes of Ghana but he did not go beyond the fact that man is a creature of a Supreme Being. That little literature exists about the tribes in Ghana on this topic may be attributed to the fact that scholars from non-Akan speaking tribes see their concept reflected in what is already written on the concept of man in the Akan traditional system. In the Akan traditional system as well as those other traditional systems in Ghana the individual is seen as a ***communal being***. For this reason, one can agree with Kwasi Wiredu, when he writes about the Ghanaian traditional concept as follows:

> *an individual is social not only because he or she lives in a community, which is*

believed to be the only context in which full development, or indeed any sort of human development is possible, but also because, by his original constitution, a human being is part of a social whole. The underlying doctrine is the belief that an individual consists of three elements. One of these comes directly from God and is in fact, a speck of the divine substance. This is the life principle. In virtue of this constituent all human beings are one and therefore are all members of the universal family of humankind whose head and spring is God. Nipa nyinaa ye Nyame mma: obiara nnye asaase ba meaning all human beings are the children of God; none is the child of the earth. The other remaining elements are more mundane in origin. There is what might be called the blood principle which comes from the mother and somewhat more stipulatively, there is what might be called the charisma principle which comes from the father. The blood from the mother is what principally gives rise to a person's body. The biological input from the father is responsible for the degree of personal presence that each individual develops at the appropriate stage. (Wiredu, 1992, p. 196)

Sarpong in his explanation of man also made mention of certain material and spiritual elements that made up the individual person. They are "*blood from the mother a spirit from the father and the soul and the breath of life from God*" (Sarpong, 1974, p.36). He pointed out however that in some societies the elements that go in to make the human person are many more than the four he has mentioned. It should be noted that for many other thinkers other slightly different explanations may exist for the elements he puts forward. (Wiley, 1981). In any case, the community significance of these components to the individual remains. Both the maternal and paternal contributions to the make-up of an individual are the bases of his membership in specific social units. So in the traditional thought system an individual has a well-structured social identity even before birth. Thus, when an adage points out that when a human being descends from on high he or she alights in a town, the idea is that one comes into a community in which one already has well defined social affiliations with society and rules and moral.

Essentially an individual is circled with obligations and responsibilities matched by rights and privileges revolving round levels of relationships irradiating from the consanguinity of household kith and kin, through the "blood" ties of lineage and clan, to the wider circumference of human familyhood based on the common possession of the divine spark. Greatest value is therefore attached to communal belonging. And the way in which a sense of communal belonging is fostered in the individual is through the concentrated stress on kinship identity. The communalistic orientation of the society in question means that an individual's image will depend rather crucially upon the extent to which his or her actions benefit others than himself, not, of course, by accident or coincidence but by design. The conception of an individual is one who through mature reflection and steady motivation is able to carve out a reasonably ample livelihood for self, "family" and a potentially wide group of kin dependents, besides making substantial contributions to the well-being of society at large. An individual who remained content with self-regarding successes would be viewed as so circumscribed in outlook as not to merit the title of a real person. (*American Peoples Encyclopedia*, p. 238)

We see that the individual is therefore composed of a complex whole of various constituents derived from ***the mother***, ***the father***, and ***the Supreme Being***. Defending the communitarian nature of the individual, Dzobo (1992, pp. 124-132) takes his point of departure from the fact that "to a considerable degree human motivations can be said to be the same for people in all cultures with varying contextual modifications and emphasis". This for him will include "*the physiologically determined drives which comprises of such master drives as hunger, thirst and sex and their derivatives; and the trans-survival drives such as the need for security, peace, safety, love, recognition, status, honour, influence, happiness, solidarity, human creativity and productivity, motherhood, fatherhood, success and prosperity*" (Dzobo, 1992, pp.124-132). He thinks that it is usually what people consider to be the basic and ultimate moving force of human behaviour that differentiates one culture from another and also reveals the true common identity of any two cultures. He conceived of the individual as a creator being with polar elements basic to his nature, a subject, and not an object of history, not evaluative, but with conflicting tendencies original to his nature and the fact that the individual is a communal being. For him reality includes the reality of man and society, structured as unity in duality comprising two conflicting elements. One important deduction from the fact that polarity has been woven into the fabric of the universe and of society is that community belongs to the very being of the individual. For him the origin of all being is existence in a polar relation. The individual's being emerges from a prior social whole which is truly other; it comes into being for the sake of him and exists for his development and growth. Hence, an individual who is cut off from the communal organism is nothing. (Mbiti, 1981). As pointed out above, as far as Africans are concerned, the reality of the communal world takes precedence over the reality of the individual life histories, whatever these may be. From this assumption, Menkiti (1984, p.171) infers that in the African view, it is the community which defines the individual not some isolated static quality of rationality, wills or memory (Abraham, 1992). This is confirmed by Gyekye (1992, p.111) when he explains that, in the communal setting of the African life, an individual's social status is measured in terms of, (i) his sense of responsibility, expressed in turn through his responsiveness and sensitivity to the needs and demands of the group; (ii) what he has been able to achieve through his own exertions - physical, intellectual, moral; and (iii) the extent to which he fulfils certain social norms such as having marital life and bringing up children (Mbiti, 1969; p.104).

It should be made clear, however, that besides being a communitarian being by nature, the individual is also by nature other things as well. By '*other things*', Gyekye (1992, p.111) means *essential attributes of the individual such as rationality, having a capacity for virtue and for evaluating and making moral judgments.* He thinks that it is not the community that creates these attributes but rather it discovers and nurtures them. For him it is true that the whole gamut of values and practices in which the individual is necessarily embedded is a creation of cultural community and is part of its history. For this reason, it can be said that some of our goals are set by the communal structure. He argues that it is not possible for the communal structure to set the whole or a seamless complex of the values, practices, and ends of the individual that will perfectly reflect the complexity of human nature. Values and practices at least, some of which we know do change cannot be considered monolithic. He explains further that the communal, and therefore cultural character of the self really does not imply that the self is ineluctably and permanently held in thrall by that structure. Moreover, the ethos of the communal structure does not pre-empt or permanently nip in the bud a possibly radical perspective on communal values and practices that may be adopted by a self. The reason for him is that since the individual participates in the shared values and practices, and is enmeshed in the web of communal relationships, he is capable of realising that aspects of those cultural givens are clumsy, undignifying or unenlightening and can thoughtfully be questioned and evaluated. The evaluation may result in the individual's affirmation or amending or refining of existing communal goals, values and practices. But it may or could also result in the individual's total rejection of them. This possibility of re-evaluation means, surely, that the individual cannot be absorbed by the communal or cultural apparatus completely, but can to some extent wriggle himself out of it, distance himself from it, and thus be in a position to take another look at it. It also means that the communal structure cannot foreclose the meaningfulness and reality of the quality of self-assertiveness, which the person can demonstrate in his actions. He explains that the development of human, i.e., communal culture results therefore from the exercise by individual persons of this capacity for self-assertion. It is this capacity which makes possible the intelligibility of autonomous individual choice of goals and life plans. The capacity for self-assertion, which the individual can exercise, presupposes, and in fact derives from the autonomous nature of the person, where autonomy does not mean self-completeness, but the acquisition of a will, a rational will of one's own, a will that enables one to determine at least some of his goals and to pursue them (Sarpong, 1974, p.112; Gyekye, 1992, p.104).

Community and the individual

In order to understand the community's influence on the individual it will be appropriate we look at certain features of this community. As pointed out above one can identify numerous tribes in Ghana. The uses and definitions of the term 'tribe' in the sociological and anthropological literature are varied and conflicting. For some authors, it means a people with a *common language*; for some others it means a people with *common culture*; for another group a people with *ancestral lineages*; and for yet another group it is a people with *common government or rulers*. Because of its many uses and connotations the term 'tribe' anthropologists have never satisfied when it is used (Mbiti, 1969, p. 105). The American Peoples Encyclopedia (1968, p.238) sees a tribe as *a primitive social group sharing a common territory, a distinct language or dialect, a common culture, and a sense of social solidarity against outsiders.* It sees tribal organization as one of the earliest forms of social and political systems. The tribe is usually divided into a number of subgroups, including the sib, which consisted of all persons believed to be descended from a common ancestor. These groups are, at different times and places, both exogamous, permitting marriage with only those outside the group, and endogamous, permitting marriage only between group members. According to some theorists, the earliest tribes developed as two or more families united for purposes of hunting, gathering, common defence and so forth. In the tribal system, economic, religious, educational, and recreational institutions are usually integrated into a comprehensive pattern of acceptable conduct. Members of most tribes are greatly dependent upon nature for survival. Each family constituted a self-subsistent unit. Land is either held in common by all members or owned by individuals or families. Personally owned possessions included clothing, tools, and dwelling places. Usually skills, customs, and mores are learned through casual, personal contact, and other knowledge is gained through ceremony and special instruction. Religion is usually of a primitive form, including animistic, pantheistic beliefs. The above conception of the tribe is not different from how scholars in Ghana and Africa understand their tribes. For Mbiti (1969, p. 105), because in recent years, the English use of the word 'tribe' has increasingly acquired semi-bad connotations, he prefers to substitute the term 'peoples' for tribes. He distinguishes one people from another among others by language, geographical region, a common history and a common culture. That there are diversities of culture in Ghana is a fact that needs no argument. Abraham (1992) thinks that the diversity of cultures attests to the richness of human creativity and invention, and he asserts that in addition to pragmatic necessity, there is empirical justification for considering Ghanaian cultural phenomena across wide areas. As a matter of fact, it is easy to be unduly impressed by the sheer number of ethnic groups, each endowed with its own cultural heritage, and overlook the repetitive elements and manifestations, which they contain. Categories of such repetitive elements include belief systems and relations between arts on the one hand, and on the other hand political, economic, religious, and familial institutions and practice, social stratification and political systems, other specific institutions and basic rules for counting descent.

This common culture also expresses itself in the form of common customs, morals, ethics, social behaviour and material objects like musical instruments, household utensils, foods and domestic animals. Thus one can comfortably say that even though there are diversities of culture, fundamental concepts like the belief in God, existence of the spirits, continuation of human life after death, magic and witchcraft, are common to all. Equally so, are concepts of the family, age groups, special persons in society, marriage customs, traditional forms of government, political personages and the like that are not very different from one tribe to the other.

The Clan

Tribes in Ghana, like many in Africa, are divided into groups technically called clans. The number of clans differs from tribe to tribe. Clans may be patrilineal or matrilineal. Membership of patrilineal clans is derived from the male line, while membership of matrilineal clans is acquired through the female line. Inheritance, succession, status, is lineally determined. Members of one clan are held to be related to one another and bound together by a common tie. This tie is the belief that all members of the clan descend from one ancestor or ancestress. Hence, members of one clan are held to be relatives, brothers, sisters, mothers, fathers, etc. They are therefore forbidden to marry, irrespective of the degree of relationship, or the spatial distance separating them (Sarpong, 1974, p. 10). Clans are normally totemic, that is, each has an animal or part of it, a plant, a stone or mineral, which is regarded as sacred. Members of a particular clan observe special care in treating or handling their totem. For example, they would not kill or eat it. The totem is *the visible symbol of unity, of kinship, of belongingness, of togetherness and common affinity* (Oduyoye, n. d.). Clan systems provide closer human co-operation, especially in times of need. In case of internal conflicts, clan members join one another to fight their aggressive neighbours. If a person finds himself in difficulties, it is not unusual for him to call for help from his clan members and other relatives, e.g. in paying fines caused by an accident or in finding enough goods to exchange for a wife. Bereavement is one of the severest trials of the human psyche, and unfortunately, it is recurrent. When it occurs, by both precept and practice, everyone in the lineage is expected to play his part by word, song, and dance and material resource. The culture does not leave this to the lineage alone. Friends, neighbours and even indirect acquaintances can always be counted upon to help in various ways to lighten the burden of sorrows. In some societies, clans have their separate land areas, while in other societies the clans are intermingled throughout the tribal land. It is the true land owning body; it holds the land in perpetuity and has no power to alienate it in part or in whole. The clan regulates production, and constitutes a political and supreme religious body, which apportions social responsibility to lineage groups and determines fields of succession.

Differences between the assigned responsibilities cause some lineage groups to take precedence over others in the succession to political and religious offices. Likewise, although each clan is entrusted with special responsibilities of state, the differences between the social and political offices and duties create differences in prestige and status between clans. Although in theory, a clan must ensure the welfare of each member, actual solicitude regarding this in practice falls on members of the household (Sarpong, 1974, p.12).

. *The family*

In Ghana, the family has a much wider circle of members in the traditional set up than the word suggests in Europe or North America. The family includes children, parents, grandparents, uncles, aunts, brothers and sisters who may have their own children, and other immediate relatives and departed relatives. Surviving members must not forget the departed. Failure to observe this results in the fear that misfortune will strike them or their relatives. Hence, food and libation are offered to them from time to time as tokens of the fellowship, communion, remembrance, respect and hospitality. The living-dead solidifies and mystically binds together the whole family. The family also includes the unborn members who are still in the loins of the living. They are the buds of hope and expectation, and each family makes sure that its own existence is not extinguished. The family provides for its continuation, and prepares for the coming of those not yet born. For that reason, parents are anxious to see that their children find husbands and wives to bring forth children. Failure to do so will mean the extinction of the family as a whole. The family, therefore, ensures an individual's civic existence. This is the most significant circle of relations, for it was through the head of the lineage that, in traditional times, a person had his political representation. For many practical purposes, however, it is the household and (basic) lineage circles of relations that have the most significance in terms of informal rights and obligations. (Sarpong, 1974, p.14). This household consists of children, parents and sometimes grandparents. It is what is referred to as *'the family at night'* for it is generally at night that the household is really itself. At night, parents are with their immediate children in the same house; they discuss private affairs of their household, and parents educate their children in matters pertaining to domestic relationships (Mbiti, 1991, p.107). The institution of family life is universal to all human cultures and the needs, which it is primed to serve, are among the deepest seething in the human psyche. Like many other parts of the world, in Ghana, this institution creates a constant and well-understood social framework for the nurturing of the young until maturity. It establishes a hospitable and forgiving atmosphere in which the young can safely and securely train for eventual social responsibilities and intercourse. It also provides a regulated and protective framework for the responsible advancement of sexual life.

Religion

The individual African sees religion as the basic reality to connect with the Supreme Being. Mbiti (1969, p. 181) was right in saying that "for Africans it (i.e. religion) is an ontological phenomenon; it pertains to the question of existence or being". The belief in the Supreme Being, lesser gods, ancestors, charms and amulets give the individual the African identity. For the Ghanaian individual, the quest to find his place in the society places value and meaning on the name given to him at birth. Religion indeed as the etymology *religare* depicts, binds the individual to obligations ontologically expected from him because of the cultural setting and the influence of African Traditional Religion.

The Ghanaian traditional belief system can be summed up in the diagram below.

Supreme Being

↓ ↑

Lesser gods

↓ ↑

Ancestral Spirits

↓ ↑

Charms and Amulets

The Supreme Being

The West African and for that matter the Ghanaian unquestionably believes in the existence of a Supreme Being. This Supreme Deity is regarded as far greater than any other being. He has different names from one tribe to the other but the qualities attributed to him are everywhere almost identical. According to Sarpong (1998, pp.21-22), anyone, who wants to understand the people's belief in such a Being, has only to make a study of any African or Ghanaian language, and it will not take him long to discover that names for this Being keep cropping up. Among the Akans of Ghana, he will hear names such as *Onyame, Onyankopon,* etc. and among the Ewes of Ghana, he will hear *Mawu.* An analysis of the names will reveal the wealth of ideas a particular people have about the Being. The immediacy of God in the affairs of Ghanaians is also demonstrated through the God-related names they bear. Theophorous names like *Nyamekye (gift of God)* and *Dardom (depend on God)* are examples of Akan names. *Mawusi (in God's hands)*, *Mawulawoe (God will accomplish it)*, *Elikplim (God is with me)* are some examples of Ewe names. ((Sarpong, 1974, p.10). In everyday speech and talk, the name of this Being is mentioned. Allusions to Him are found in ordinary wise sayings and proverbs and are written on vehicles, stores, doors and public places of importance. He is thought of as a being in the sky but His presence is felt everywhere and He sees everything. He is the creator and provider of all that we need. He is a Supreme Being who is kind, fatherly, loving, and eternal. He is a judge, the giver of water, the giver of light and what have you. He is experienced as the good parent, the grandparent, *Nana,* a source of loving-kindness and protection. Some say *Nana* is a male and so they address the Being as father, while others say *Nana* is a female and so they address the Being as mother. But the sentiment expressed about the Being is the same. Ghanaians experience their 'closeness' to the Being, and therefore use the terms 'mother' and/or 'father' to give a description based upon what they see the Being doing in their lives. Many Ghanaians see the Being as a great Being, and so the Akan say: *Nsa baako ntumi nkata Onyame ani* meaning no single hand can cover the eye of God. To the Ghanaian, God is incomprehensible, He is invisible, and He cannot be represented in any way. He scarcely has temples and priests. Hence, according to Sarpong (1974, p. 12), *"...sacrifices to God, while not being altogether lacking are a rare occurrence; so also is what one may term public worship. He seldom has priests. If worship is defined in terms of temples and priests, then little worship is given to God. Rarely are temples built for him. Images of God are almost non-existent...the (African) will laugh if one spoke of the possibility of representing God".*

As the Creator and continuous Originator, public sacrifices, even when they are offered to idols and the ancestors, are not without his invocation. He is usually invoked before everyone.

3.2.3.2. Personal Theophoric Names

Names have powerful effects on the individual and there are many traditional African names derived from the concept of the Supreme Being. The existence of the Supreme Being and the attachment that individuals have with Supreme Being make them give these theophoric names to themselves and their children. These personal names are compounded with God's name. These theophoric names show how further real God is to the African (Quarcoopome, 1987, p. 33). The concept of the Supreme Being is revealed in the very names that Ghanaians also pride themselves with. These names sometimes empower individuals to act according to the meaning and connotation of them. Individuals like their names try and are convinced to act out these names. Personal theophoric names usually have impact on persons who bear them and they bring out feelings and 'religiosity' in these persons.

Consequently, "when prayers are answered after urgent supplications to God as in the case of prolonged childlessness or for any other event or happening, then in gratitude for benefits and blessings received, theophoric names are given, to children born within this period" (ibid., p. 33). Examples of these names are *Nyamekye* 'The Gift of God', *Mawunyo* (God is Kind), *Mawuenyega* (God is the greatest One), *Selasi* (God/Nature hears). These names derived from personal experience with the Supreme Being, help individuals to look back to their experiences and motivate themselves in times of difficulties. There are also names that express African ideas of reincarnation. Ancestors are believed to be born into families so that they can complete an unfinished work or calling. Hence the Akan name *Ababio* means 'He has come back'. Individuals are empowered to act in similar way as their ancestors who once lived. It brings out the vigour and the vitality which names erupt in us. Therefore, personal theophoric names express belief in the Supreme Being and how an individual is empowered to act out that name which he or she bears.

Lesser gods

There is also belief in the existence of a body of spirits created by the Supreme Being. The existence of these minor gods everywhere in Africa is a fact which needs no formal proof. According to Sarpong (1974, p.14), they range from great tribal gods to little private deities and fall roughly into one of the four groups below.

1. Those generally worshipped by one tribe. These traditional general deities are few in number.

2. Those worshipped by inhabitants of certain towns, localities or traditional area. These are the local deities. They are very numerous, every locality having several.

3. Those worshipped by the smaller sections of the community such as special lineages or village companies. Every lineage or family has its own deity of this class.

4. Those worshipped each day by one individual or his household. In practice, the individual, since he

is a member of a tribe, a community, a lineage and a family, is subject to gods from all the groups.

They are supposed to possess astonishing powers. Even though they are creatures of the Supreme Being and subordinate to Him, they may use their enormous powers independent of Him either to the advantage of man or to his detriment, when the need arises. They seem to have love for those residential areas which induce fear and reverence and they have as their earthly abode, anything from rivers to creepers, and from beasts to rocks or mountains. They may be male or female, but their influence is independent of their sex. Not every god is benevolent to man, some indeed are, but others are mischievous. The importance of the lesser gods is commensurate with the kind of need that they are supposed to provide for their subjects. Tribal deities are first in the order of precedence, followed by divisional ones. Further still, more importance is attached to deities of chiefdoms than to those whose influence extends over a village or lineage. They are said to have means of supplying the needs of their subjects. They demand worship and obedience from man in default of which they inflict punishment on him. Consequently, sacrifices are made to them either to repay the benignity of the good ones or to avoid the malignity of the ill-disposed ones. They are believed to be endowed with power to bless and kill. However, they kill only when their sanctioned laws and prohibitions have been violated or when they are invoked to do so. They have shrines and priests who offer sacrifices to them. Through their priests and priestesses, they can foretell the future, prevent evil, provide antidotes against certain sicknesses, make ill-luck befall people who do not obey them and protect those who worship them.

Ancestors

There is also the strong belief in the influence of the spirit of the good dead-relatives on the living. They are believed to inhabit a special world of ghosts or spirits. Not all the dead relatives are considered ancestors. To qualify as an ancestor, one should have attained adulthood and should have married and had children. One should have died a natural death, i.e. not through accident or certain diseases. Under certain circumstances those who die in action i.e. in war fighting for the people are also accepted as ancestors. The Ghanaian thinks he can call them and tell them things or offer them food and drink. The dead are supposed to partake invisibly in the life of this world. They continue the ties of relationship and kinship after death. The living therefore are most anxious to keep good relations with their dead relatives, to remember them, to show concern for them, to be one with them, and to ask for help and favours from them. Those, who for any reason or the other, do not qualify as ancestors are reincarnated. It must be noted that it is not only those who are unable to enter the world of the ancestors that are reborn. There is the strong belief that any ancestor who thinks his work on earth was not completed before his death may decide to come back to complete it. Even though they do not feel the kind of pain which our bodies experience, ancestors can be sorrowful, as for instance when the living break their laws or taboos. Among them there are no deformed persons. A man without a leg or an arm will get it back when he enters the place of the dead. In the world of the ancestors, there is status and rank, and inferiors have to obey their superiors. At the place of the dead he is supposed to lead exactly the life that he led whiles on earth. For example, if he was a chief on earth, he remains a chief after his death. Even though the living cannot go to the world of ancestors, they believe that the ancestors keep a close and constant contact with the living members of their lineage. They are sometimes supposed to visit the living. Normally, nobody sees them, but it is said that certain people possess visionary gifts and are able to see them. The Ghanaian is constantly preoccupied with the thought that the ancestors are watching him. This preoccupation serves to regulate his daily life and behaviour. This thought is a very potent sanction to morality. Although ancestors receive their power from the Supreme Being, they use it independent of him. They may be benevolent or malevolent. They are makers, guardians and custodians of tribal laws. They obtain favours from God and send help to their relatives. One ancestor may indicate to one of his own people the remedy to an illness in his dream; another one may send material things such as money, among others; and yet another may see to it that the girls of his lineage are endowed. Contacts are made to them by means of sacrifice, libation and prayer. Therefore, one can be an ancestor to a particular lineage, clan or town and sometimes tribes.

Charms and Amulets

The Ghanaian also believes in charms and amulets. This group of deities are separated from the other group in the sense that they are articles of some kind, which are worn or hanged in the house for protective purposes (Sarpong, 1974, p. 15). If, on one hand, one considers the fact that there is only an acknowledged creator who holds sway over all other beings, then one is right to conclude that the ATR is monotheistic. But if on the other hand, other deities and spirits, to whom public cult is directed, are taken into consideration, then one can conclude with some measure of justification that it is polytheistic.

Features of the Tribal System

To survive, the tribal members believe that they must allow the wisest member among them to make major decisions for them. In some tribes, the chief must be the strongest member. Allowing the tribe to be led by a physically strong leader is thought to be the most efficient method of organization because it places responsibility upon one person who will allow no division or dissent. This strong person will, through his leadership and power, presumably transfer that strength to the other members of the tribe. Loyalty to the tribe is a cardinal requirement of any tribal member. The tribe cannot survive, if there is dissent among any of its members. When survival is as precarious as they find it, then dissent is traitorous. Anyone who does not exhibit loyalty to the tribe is an evil outsider who challenges the deity, casts evil spells, and does not believe in the special character of the tribe. This makes this person an enemy worthy of death or defeat. A clear distinction is made between *"we and the others"*. Sometimes some members are seen as enemies; at other times they are seen as inferior personalities. The tribe also has solidarity in ideas. Each member must believe in the same god, must have the same ideas, and work toward the same goals. The purpose for this is that, when individuals in a group hold the same beliefs, the leader can appeal to ideas that would foster the "survival" of the tribe. A collective "will" is developed that presumably makes the tribe stronger. For them the universe is antithetical to man and scarcity breeds the need for struggle. Hence, tribal solidarity is essential. The thought processes are wholly group based. Every thought is of "we," every injunction is a duty for "us," every enemy is "our" enemy; every god is "our" god, every belief, "our" belief. There is simply no such idea as the individual and to question anything held by the group is a complete impossibility. Even a personal wish, if any exists, is rationalized as a wish to help others. Ritual practices allow for the release of physical energy and the pooling of that energy toward the goals of the tribe. The goal of ritual practice is not only to impart a moral theme (laws) handed down from the gods, but also to allow each person the opportunity to declare himself a member of the tribe. Ritual practices allow each person to fit into the collective and thereby to judge himself a fully-fledged rightful member. Ritual joining and collective cultural paradigms involve the "acting out" of ancient myths, which are achieved by constant repetition of actions or words. Such joining makes the person feel that since he does the same thing others do equally well, then he must be all right; he is good. Most often such rituals are not difficult to imitate. This communitarian ethos of the African culture is also echoed in the works of some African novelists. Clearly, then, the African social structures with its underlying socio-ethical philosophy was and is still communitarian.

The Individual and Its Relationship with the Community

From the above we realised that the stress on the ontological primacy of the community, the natural sociality of the individual, the organic character of the relations between individuals, and the all-importance of the community for the total well-being or complete realization of the nature of the individual seem to be the main factor that defines the individual and his relationship to the society. As has been pointed out above, *Ghanaian societies are pre-existing networks into which individuals are born.* We observe that these networks define relations that their new members are to bear to one another, and relations through whom their personal growth is to be nurtured and sustained. In these cultures, the members are nurtured on common beliefs, ranges of values, attitudes, and actions, which are supposed to make life in their society orderly. Through the same cultures, the members are believed to acquire skills and develop initiatives, by which life in society becomes satisfying. This resulted in the belief that the individual in the traditional society does not and cannot exist alone except corporately. He owes his existence to other people, including those of past generations and his contemporaries. He is simply part of the whole. The community is what therefore makes, creates or produces the individual. Physical birth is not seen as enough to make an individual what he will become. The child must go through rites of incorporation so that it becomes fully integrated into the entire society. These rites continue throughout the physical life of the person, during which the individual passes from one stage of corporate existence to another. The final stage is reached when he dies and even then he is ritually incorporated into the wider family of both the dead and the living. What we see is that in this society only in terms of other people does the individual become conscious of his own being, his own duties, his privileges and responsibilities towards himself and towards other people. When he suffers, he does not suffer alone but with the corporate group; when he rejoices, he rejoices not alone but with his kinsmen, his neighbours and his relatives, whether dead or living. Whatever happens to the individual happens to the whole group, and whatever happens to the whole group happens to the individual. Hence the individual can only say '*I am, because we are; and since we are, therefore I am*' (Mbiti, 1991, p.108). The relationship between the individual and the society is mutual and interdependent. Each has a mutual responsibility for the other. The individual is always aware that his well-being lies in the welfare of his society. He is taught to live for his society just as his society lives for him, and to cooperate with others to create a wholesome society. In other words, the individual is expected to contribute to the educative power of society which in turn helps to develop the individual's creative powers. N. K. Dzobo (1992) explains that this awareness is responsible for the unique indigenous social orientation which may be characterized as the "*we orientation.*" In the "we orientation" life is comprehended not from the perspective of 'I' or 'they' alone, but from that of both which unite to become 'we'. This 'we' comprehension of life is given expression in various forms of speech, greeting and action. For him the best symbol used to express the '*we-istic*' comprehension of life is the hand. In the symbol of the hand the fingers represent individual members of society, who are free, unique and independent. But they are firmly rooted in the whole which is the hand, and derive their being and importance from their relatedness in the whole, individually and collectively. The community, symbolized by the whole hand, derives its existence from the interrelatedness of its fingers. Without the fingers there will be no hand, without the hand there will be no fingers. Kwame Gyekye (1992, p.102) asserts that the general assumption that with its emphasis on communal values, collective good and shared ends, communitarians invariably conceive the person as wholly constituted by social relationships, and that it tends to whittle down the moral autonomy of the person and makes the being and life of the individual person totally dependent on the activities, values, projects, practices and ends of the community which consequently diminishes his freedom and capability to choose or question or re-evaluate the shared values of the community which will not go unchallenged. But the fact remains that *"as far as Africans are concerned, the reality of the communal world takes precedence over the reality of the individual life histories, whatever these may be."* The individual is seen as an inherently communal being, embedded in a context of social relationships and interdependence, never as an isolated, atomic individual. So important is the society that it is not seen as a mere association of individuals whose interests and ends are contingently congruent.

But as a group of persons linked by interpersonal bonds, biological and/or non-biological, who consider themselves primarily as members of the group and who have common interests, goals and values. The notion of common interests and values is crucial and it defines the community. Members share goals and values. They have intellectual and ideological, as well as emotional, attachments to those goals and values; as long as they cherish them, they are ever ready to pursue and defend them.

In the traditional thought system the fact that the individual is born into an existing community is evidence that the individual is by nature a social being. This individual therefore is naturally oriented toward other persons and must have relationships with them. Consequently, social relationships become necessary and not conditional. In this community, the individual does not voluntarily choose to enter into human community which implies that community life is not optional for any individual and must not live in isolation from other persons. The fundamentally relational character of the individual and the interdependence of other individuals arising out of their natural sociality are thus essential. It is this necessary relationship, which complete the being of the individual who, prior to entering into those relationships, was not self-complete. It is evidently true that in the social context, in terms of functioning or flourishing in a human community, the individual person is not self-sufficient. Ones capacities, talents and dispositions are not adequate for the realization of his potential and basic needs. The community alone is believed to constitute the context, the social or cultural space, in which the actualization of the possibilities of the individual person can take place. It is seen to provide the individual person with the opportunity to express his individuality, to acquire and develop his personality and to fully become the kind of person he wants to be. The understanding is that the system of values which the person inherits as he enters into the cultural community and the range of goals in life from which he can choose are not anterior to a cultural structure but a function of the structure itself. They are therefore posterior to the culture and the products of the community. Thus, in so far as the cultural community constitutes the context or medium in which the individual person works out and chooses his goals and life plans, and, through these activities, ultimately becomes what he wants to be, the cultural community must be held as prior to the individual.

Political Status of the Individual

Traditionally, almost all Ghanaian communities are unions of clans. The highest authority in the scheme of functions is the paramount chief or king. A king or paramount chief is distinguished strictly from the office, which he bears. The office itself is a sacred one, an object of awe and reverence, and the focus of the deepest religious performances. It is defended by a system of taboos and observances. It is the legitimizer of the hierarchy of authority and power by which the functions of the community are carried out. Abraham (1992, pp.23-24) explains that it is only derivative and not inherent that the person of the king is likewise sacred. His succession is on the basis of the consent of electors, and his continuance in office is at the sufferance of his council and his people. Without inherent power to subjugate his people or territory, his own ascendancy is entrenched by the mystique he derives from his office as a sacerdotal leader. Accordingly, he is required to be a paragon of the spiritual and moral purity of his people and a repository of their intellectual virtues and wisdom. A council of chiefs and courts surrounds the king. There is an African saying that there are no bad kings; there are only bad counsellors. From the council devolves the authority whereby families carry out their functions (Mbiti, 1969, p. 108). With the above set up, the individual derives his political authority and functions from the family which is represented in the clan and the family derives its authority and functions from the clan which is also represented at the tribal level. It might be supposed that the tribal system with its emphasis on and concern for communal values will have no truck with the doctrine of rights. But Gyekye (1992, pp.113-114) thinks that it will be false, both in theory and practice. He believes that the respect for human dignity, a natural or fundamental attribute of the individual which cannot be set at nought by the communal structure, generates regard for personal rights. The reason is that the natural membership of the individual person in a community cannot rob him of his dignity or worth, a fundamental and inalienable attribute he possesses as a person. In this case the recognition of the rights of the individual is a conceptual requirement. He asserts, however, that even though the system may not be opposed to individual rights, it may consciously and purposively give greater attention or care to other communal values of the community than to the individual.

> *It must be granted that communitarianism cannot be expected to make a fetish of rights; thus rights talk will not be brought to the front burner of its concerns and preoccupations. The reason is not far to seek; it is derivable from the logic of the communitarian theory itself: it assumes an overwhelming concern for communal values, for the good of the wider society as such… even though rights belong primarily to individuals, ….nevertheless, in so far as their exercise will often, directly or indirectly, be valuable to the larger society, their status and roles must be recognized*

> *by communitarian theory. But the theory will disallow separating rights from the common values of the community and conferring on them a pre-eminent status... in the communitarian political morality, priority will not be given to rights if doing so will stand in the way of attaining a more highly ranked value or a more preferable goal of the community. Rights would not, therefore, be held as absolute in the communitarian theory.*

He explains further that even though the communal structure will allow the exercise of

individual rights, it can be expected that it would not suggest to individuals relentlessly insisting on their rights. This is because by the nature of the communal structure rights, political, economic, and social rights are built into the ethos and practices of the cultural community. Thus, the economic, political, and social needs of the individual members, which are the concern of most individual rights, have been recognized, if not catered for, to some degree by the communitarian structure. In a social situation that stresses social relations, concern and compassion for others, and other communal values, insistence on rights may not be necessary. However, whiles the system would not have a dogmatic attitude to individual rights, it would certainly have one toward duties that individual members have or ought to have toward other members of the community. Concerned, as it is, with the common good or the communal welfare, the welfare of each and every member of the community, duty is considered as the moral tone, the supreme principle of morality which one is obliged to do. Such obligations will include helping others in distress and not to harm others, and so on. This is explained in terms of the fact that priority is based on, and is most probably required by the demands of the relational character of the person in the wake of his natural sociality. The sociality of the person immediately makes him naturally oriented to other persons with whom he must live in relation. Our natural sociality then prescribes or mandates a morality that, clearly, should be weighted on duty, i.e. on that which one has to do for others. The common good, which is an outstanding goal of the communitarian moral and political philosophy, requires that each individual should work for the good of all. The social and ethical values of social well-being, solidarity, interdependence, cooperation, compassion, and reciprocity, which can be said to characterize the communitarian morality, primarily impose on the individual a duty to the community and its members. It is all these considerations that elevate the notion of duties to a priority status in the whole enterprise of communitarian life.

In stressing duties to the community and its members rather than the rights of the individual members of the community, the communitarian theory does not imply, by any means, that rights are not important, neither does it deny duties to the self. Rights of the individual such as the right to equal treatment, to our property, to freely associate with others, to free speech, and others, would be recognized by the tribal system. However, in the light of the overwhelming emphasis on duties, rights would not be given priority over the values of duty and so would not be considered uninfringeable. For the sake of the common good it might be appropriate occasionally to override some individual rights.

Economic Status of the Individual

The traditional economy is predominantly agricultural. As pointed out above, land is owned by the clan or families. The land is further divided among members for farming activities to help provide for their households. It does not become a private property of an individual at any point in time. It is the property of the family and remains so. So by its very nature, property is communal. The individual is born into this community to be supported by it because at birth the individual is who is totally dependent upon others and therefore not self-sufficient. Through growth and acculturation, he acquires skills and abilities that reduces this dependency, but he is never able to eliminate it completely. Self-reliance is, of course, understood and recommended, but its very possibility is predicated upon this in eliminable residue of human dependency. Human beings, therefore, at all times, in one way or another, directly or indirectly, need the help of their kind. One very standard situation in which this truth was continually illustrated is in traditional agriculture. In such a mode of production, recurrent stages were easily foreseeable at which the resources of any one farmer would be insufficient to accomplish a necessary task, be it the initial clearing of the ground or the scooping out of, say, cocoa beans from great heaps of pods. In such moments, all that is necessary is for one to send word to one's neighbours indicating the time, place and the nature of help needed. The people would assemble at the right time at the indicated place with their own implements of work and together help get the job done speedily and almost with festive enthusiasm. Individuals who availed themselves of the benefits of this system and yet dragged their feet when the call comes from others are brought to conformity or branded social outcasts.

Morality and the Individual

In the traditional system good conduct is stressed and ensured and non-conformists are brought to conformity or ostracized. Kudadjie (1995) thinks morality is determined in some cases by religion but in other cases by custom and other social factors of a non-religious nature. Other scholars argue that morality is determined, not by religion, but by practical considerations regarding human welfare in society (Gyekye, 1992, pp. 115-116). Wiredu (1992, pp.63-65) thinks that in the Ghanaian tradition of philosophy, *"morality is neither purely intellectual, for it has an irreducible passional ingredient, nor purely personal, for it is essentially social"*. For the purpose of our work, however, we shall look at the cult of the ancestor as the basis of individual morality in the traditional society.

This is because the ultimate aim of the individual is to become a member of the community of the "living dead" when he dies. In line with this, Dzobo (1992, pp.231-234) argues that the English word "ancestor," meaning "one from whom one is descended and who is usually more remote in the line of descent than a grandparent" will not go down well with the Ghanaian thought system. For the traditional thought system, the understanding is that the ancestor is "lord" and "knight". In Christianity, he is a saint and martyr. The title "ancestor" is conferred upon those who earn it by the excellent way they conduct their lives. Ancestor is then, first and foremost, a moral title and is earned by living virtuously in this life. Once earned in this life, one takes into the other world. The patterns of the lives of the ancestors and the values and principles they cherish have become the normative standards of conduct. To help others grow and pursue this ideal life, the title ancestor "*nana* or *togbui*" is conferred upon living chiefs and elders of the society. These are considered society's moral paragons, in order to make the presence of the ancestor more apparent. The individual is therefore expected to lead a creative, productive and dignified life just like the ancestors. Consequently, the primary thrust of the ancestor institution is moral and general human creativity, even though it may contain some religious elements. The breakdown of this creative, productive and dignified life may vary from one traditional area to the other but the following criteria are common: A life worthy of emulation will require that the individual marries and brings forth children to perpetuate the family tree. Consequently, having as many children as possible is not a sign of irresponsibility but a virtue. It is a way of fulfilling an understanding of the essence of human existence that involves full participation in the creativity of humanity and the passing on of the creative power of life from one generation to another through the process of marriage and procreation.

The essence of the ideal life is creativity, which is seen as the foundation of all human existence. Morally conceived, it is a life of one never-ending process of human and communal relationship, defined primarily in terms of reciprocal obligations and rights. Flowing from this creativity-oriented view of life, the individual is viewed as a channel and part of the great creative power of life. The ultimate end of the individual is to create and realize a creative personality as an individual link in the chain of generations born and yet unborn. Another very much advocated quality is bravery. The individual is expected to be brave because the living dead are said to form a company of warriors in the other world, and so only the brave can join them there. In addition to the above factors of the exemplary life, there are some character traits, which go to make the exemplary life. The individual must not insult others, steal nor take other people's wives or husbands. He must not be a talkative, an alcoholic, or an extravagant type. The individual must not harbour malice towards others, but should be hard-working, kind, loving, pacific, respectful and merciful. One must keep one's promises, associate with good company, be truthful and be discrete. Finally, one must be hopeful, cheerful and neat. An individual who consistently manifest traits opposite to the above mentioned is not a person to be imitated and so can neither be an ancestor nor enjoy eternity. It is interesting to note that wealth does not qualify or disqualify a person from becoming an ancestor. It is the use of wealth that determines whether its owner should be called an ancestor or not. It is the generous use of wealth that is always encouraged. The individual in the indigenous society is therefore taught from early childhood to share whatever he has with others, both the living and the living dead, especially food. Thus, ancestral ceremonies do not constitute a worship of dead grandparents, but rather a devotion to the loftiest spiritual values of creative humanity as well as the value of sociality which is realized only through a creative dialectical tension between the *I* and *Thou*. The reverential attitude to the ancestors is a way of conceptualizing the ideal life.

Shortcomings

The tribal system derives some kind of consolation from slogans such as no man is an island unto himself, men should help each other, work together to solve social problems and the like. But scholars believe that collectivism has devastated more lives than one can imagine. That uncontrolled collectivism responsible for most of the evil that humanity has brought into this world during historical times is a scandalous omission seldom discussed. This is made evident in the Western world when the philosophers of Enlightenment reinvented collectivism to retain the elements of ritualism, converting the tribes into races or nations and attaching a modern philosophical flavour to the old fundamentals. In this development, the tribal chief becomes the government or dictator. Like the tribal chief, the collective must have someone whose views represent the collective mind, someone with the prestige and power to transfer the collective goals into action. Collectivism empowers one individual who makes its myths real and can affect the survival of the group. In a wider sense, collectivism fosters dictatorship because the members believe that the will of the group is best implemented by the will of one person. For our purposes, it is important to recognize that a philosophy that fosters a collective identity as a primary component necessarily must foster an unthinking acceptance by the individual. This leads to passivity and opens the door to dictatorship. The dictator does not want confident, happy individuals living in freedom without fear. He wants unhappy, fearful, humble, obedient and unassuming automatons. Necessarily, the collective will train its members early about the value of sacrifice and the guilt that they must feel if they challenge the collective. This idea pits a person against himself and is responsible for many of the psychological problems of modern man. Only debilitating mediocrity or rebellious non-participation can be the outcome of a situation where the individual must sacrifice his mind, his work, his ability to the will of the leader. It is the cause of the decay that afflicts most collectivist societies. Unlike the above, the philosophy of individualism fosters the independence of the individual so it would necessarily foster a form of government and society that gives the individual choice and dignity. Each person would be able to question the views and actions of the leaders of society and would be a deterrent against the formation of dictatorship.

The ant, it seems, is the perfect automaton. It lives solely for the sake of the colony. It operates automatically and everything it does is designed to advance the collective. The ant performs its duty without aberration and without any semblance of volitional control. It simply does what it is supposed to do. The belief is that if only man were able to see himself as part of the greater whole, as only an instrument through which the group is able to survive, then we would have a perfect society. If only man would do what he is supposed to do, then we can live in peace forever. This view, which is part and parcel of the collectivist view of man, indicates how strongly efforts are in collectivist societies to instil group loyalty and devotion. The individual is required to possess only one form of identity, a collective identity, because only this view will perpetuate the goals of the collective. An individual identity would necessarily negate the collective and destroy it, just as one rogue ant would cause harm to the entire colony. This is because a collectivist sees his group as the only true representative of humanity. Postulating evil enemies helps motivate the members of the collective to fight for the goals of the group. The collective therefore keeps a stream of propaganda flowing against any other group. Prejudice, over generalization, and lies are its infectious tools. It also does everything possible to whip up a common paranoia, collective pride, collective identity and collective superiority. This is why warfare is inevitable in a collectivist society. Inevitably, the collective must engage in a struggle for world dominance. The greater and more sinister the enemies, the greater must be the struggle against them, the more hated they must be, and the more cruel the effort to eradicate them. The role of the individual is to sacrifice for others, be meek and humble before God, fear God, follow commandments or he will end up in tortuous hell for eternity. Men are taught to fight their sexual and worldly natures and feel guilty for experiencing pleasure. Free will is the idea that in morality each human being has a choice to do either right or what becomes wrong later. It asserts that when a person must make a choice between different courses of action, he can freely choose the course he will take after analysing the facts. More fundamentally, free will holds that man must choose to engage his mind in the thinking that will secure his survival. This implies a mind capable of evaluating reality and of reasoning and decision-making. It further holds that man can either initiate the process of thinking or he can evade that choice and let chance determine the correctness of a particular course of action. It assumes that man is clean morally and capable of correct action. It assumes that he can improve his life by making the correct choices. It provides the foundation for a true self-esteem, since self-esteem is an outgrowth, fundamentally, of a properly reasoning mind. Free will functions best in the independent mind, the mind not encumbered by fear of the collective and all the physical discomforts that this fear is seen to create. The collectivist is a person whose capacity for free will, clear thinking, is distorted by fear of the collective. Anytime fear is a factor in moral choice, a person becomes motivated by the fear rather than the requirements of reality and virtually anything goes. To be constantly focused on what other people require, what other people think is to have a corrupted capacity for proper choice. A person with this focus becomes a victim of whims and emotions, distorted as they might be, and does not have the full capacity to make rational judgments. The person who feels compelled to ask others what is the proper thing to do is an "*otherist*".

Conclusion

The tribal theory, which considers the community as a fundamental human good, advocates a life lived in harmony and cooperation with others, a life of mutual consideration and aid and of interdependence, a life in which one shares in the fate of the other, bearing one another up in a life which provides a viable framework for the fulfilment of the individual's nature or potentials, a life in which the products of the exercise of an individual's talents or endowments are regarded as the assets of the community as such. We have, however, realised that even though the individual in African social and political philosophy cannot be permanently detached from his contingent communal features, he is fully embedded or implicated in the life of his community. Nevertheless, from time to time, one can by virtue of or by exploiting one's other natural attributes essential to his metaphysical constitution, take a distanced view of his communal values and practices and reassess or revise them. This possibility implies that the self can set some of his goals and, in this way, participate in the determination or definition of his own identity. It is not surprising, therefore, that when new social, economic, moral and political thought systems such as the Western thought system were introduced into the community, the individual was influenced. The influence, which the Western thought system exercised over the traditional system in their encounter is our concern in the next chapter.

CHAPTER FOUR

THE ENCOUNTER WITH THE WEST

Introduction

After we have looked at the place of the individual in the supposedly ideal traditional society, we shall now turn our attention to his encounter with the Western thought system and how it transforms him. Through historical analyses we shall look at the interaction in economic life, political life, social life, and religious life, among others. We shall then consider briefly the importance of the encounter with particular reference to its advantages and shortcomings as far as the society is concerned and end with its impact on the individual.

Trade

According to *Ghana: History* (*Ghana, Country Study*, 1967, p. 208), under the topic *Early European Contact and the Slave Trade*, when the first Europeans arrived in the late fifteenth century, many inhabitants of the Gold Coast area were striving to consolidate their newly acquired territories and to settle into a secure and permanent environment. By 1471, under the patronage of Prince Henry the Navigator, the Portuguese arrived at the area that was to become known as the Gold Coast. This area is known to the Europeans as the source of gold that reached Muslim North Africa by way of trade routes across the Sahara. The Portuguese interest in trading for gold, ivory, and pepper increased so much so that in 1482 they built their first permanent trading post on the western coast of present-day Ghana. This fortress, which today is known as the Elmina Castle, was constructed to protect Portuguese trade from European competitors and hostile Africans. Their position on the Gold Coast remained secure for almost a century. During this period, Lisbon leased the right to establish trading posts to individuals or companies that sought to align themselves with the local chiefs and to exchange trade goods. They had both the rights to conduct commerce and trade in slaves whom the chiefs could provide.

During the seventeenth and eighteenth centuries, when first some Dutch, and later some English, some Danes, and some Swedes were granted licenses by their governments to trade overseas, fortified trade stations were built on the Gold Coast by these European competitors to challenge the Portuguese. Sometimes they were also drawn into conflicts with local inhabitants as they developed commercial alliances with local chiefs. The principal early struggle was between the Dutch and the Portuguese. With the loss of Elmina in 1642 to the Dutch, the Portuguese left the Gold Coast permanently. The next 150 years was marked by local conflicts and diplomatic manoeuvres, during which various European powers struggled to establish or to maintain a position of dominance in the profitable trade. More forts were built, abandoned, attacked, captured, sold, and exchanged, and many sites were selected at one time or another for fortified positions by contending European nations. Both the Dutch and the British formed companies to advance their African ventures and to protect their coastal establishments. The Dutch West India Company operated throughout most of the eighteenth century. The British African Company of Merchants, founded in 1750, was the successor to several earlier organizations of this type. These enterprises built and manned new installations as the companies pursued their trading activities and defended their respective jurisdictions with varying degrees of government backing. There were short-lived ventures by the Swedes and the Prussians. The Danes remained until 1850, when they withdrew from the Gold Coast. The British gained possession of the Dutch coastal forts by the last quarter of the nineteenth century, and became the dominant European power on the Gold Coast.

Trade in Slave

It is claimed that slavery and slave trading were already firmly entrenched in many African societies before their contact with Europe. In most situations, men as well as women captured in local warfare became slaves. In general, however, slaves in African communities were often treated as junior members of the society with specific rights, and many were ultimately absorbed into their masters' families as full members. The European encounter with Ghana through trade in slave was a response to the opening of European plantations in the New World during the 1500s, which suddenly expanded the demand for slaves in the Americas. Trade in slaves soon overshadowed gold and other items as the principal export. Indeed, the west coast of Africa became the principal source of slaves for the New World and the seemingly insatiable market and the substantial profits to be gained from the slave trade attracted adventurers from all over Europe. Curtin (1972) estimates that roughly 6.3 million slaves were shipped from West Africa to North America and South America, about 4.5 million of that number between 1701 and 1810. Perhaps 5,000 a year were shipped from the Gold Coast alone. All nations with an interest in West Africa participated in the slave trade. Relations between the Europeans and the local populations were often strained, and distrust led to frequent clashes. Disease caused high losses among the Europeans engaged in the slave trade, but the profits realized from the trade continued to attract them.

Abolition of the Slave Trade

The growth of anti-slavery sentiment among Europeans made slow progress against vested African and European interests that were reaping profits from the traffic.

Although individual clergymen condemned the slave trade as early as the seventeenth century, major Christian denominations did little to further early efforts at abolition. *The Quakers*, however, publicly declared themselves against slavery as early as 1727. Later in the century, the Danes stopped trading in slaves; Sweden and the Netherlands soon followed. The importation of slaves into the United States was outlawed in 1807. In the same year, Britain used its naval power and its diplomatic muscle to outlaw trade in slaves by its citizens and to begin a campaign to stop the international trade in slaves. These efforts, however, were not successful until the 1860s because of the continued demand for labour on the plantation in the New World. Webster, Boahen & Tidy (1980) think that *Britain abolished the Atlantic slave trade because of economic and humanitarian reasons.* This, they identified as the industrial revolution and the evangelical revival. They explain that in the last quarter of the eighteenth century, Britain became more interested in the new cotton and palm oil trades, which supported the industrial revolution taking place in England. Raw cotton was needed for Britain's new textile factories and palm oil was needed to lubricate factory machinery. The industrialists wanted ships to go directly to the USA and return with raw cotton, and wanted ships loaded with British manufactured cotton to go to West Africa and return directly with palm oil. The slave trade interfered with the palm oil trade in West Africa because European slave traders paid higher prices than oil traders. Often therefore oil traders were made to wait as long as a year for a cargo, while they rushed to meet the slave traders' requirements. This pushed up the cost of oil, which the industrialists in Britain had to pay, and it reduced their profits. To abolish the slave trade means quick delivery of oil and higher profits for industrialists in Britain. On the humanitarian front it was observed that in the last quarter of the eighteenth century an evangelical revival took place in Britain. There was a new concern among many British Christians for the welfare of all mankind, and this new spirit of humanitarianism supported the industrialists. Influenced by *evangelicalism*, many British people began to regard slavery and the slave trade as evil. The abolitionists, led by Granville Sharp, Thomas Clarkson and William Wilberforce, carried out a brilliant propaganda campaign, which so aroused British public opinion that it made the British Parliament abolish the slave trade for British subjects in 1807. In 1833 another Act of Parliament abolished slavery itself in British possessions. These measures did not stop the Atlantic slave trade. Other nations rushed in to take over where the British left off, and between 1807 and 1845 the trade flourished as never before. However, the British Government, backed by industrialists, humanitarians and missionaries, was determined that the slave trade should end entirely. A British naval squadron was therefore stationed off the coast of West Africa to seize slave ships and take the slaves to Sierra Leone, where missionaries could teach them Christianity.

Legitimate Commerce

Though the Atlantic slave trade did not die easily, by about 1850 it was in serious decline. It was being replaced by *'legitimate commerce'* the term used by nineteenth century Europeans to describe the legal trade in goods rather than slaves. The illegal trade in slaves was replaced by legitimate trade in a wide range of exports, including goods which had been exported for centuries, such as gold from the Gold Coast, gum from Senegal and ivory from various parts of the forest zone. But the most important exports in legitimate trade were the new products, palm oil and groundnut oil.

The palm oil trade, which arose in the eighteenth century, before the abolition and suppression of the slave trade, expanded in the nineteenth century to meet the greater demand for palm oil in the industrializing continents as pointed out above. As modern industry grew in Europe and North America, palm oil was needed not only to grease factory machines but also to lubricate new railway engines and to make soap and candles. Another unexpected result of the suppression of the slave trade and the rise of trade in vegetable oils was the increase in the amount of European political intervention in West Africa. West African farmers became customers for British manufactured goods. In other words, ***trade with Africans*** was now considered to be more profitable than ***trade in Africans***. This brought Europeans steadily into the political life of the coastal kingdoms, and led finally to conquest and partition.

The Process of Colonization

As pointed out above the British, through conquest or purchase, had become masters of most of the forts along the coast. The two major factors that laid the foundations for British rule and the eventual establishment of a colony on the Gold Coast are British reaction to the Asante wars which were causing instability and disrupting trade, and Britain's increasing preoccupation with the suppression and elimination of the slave trade. The invasions by the Asante disrupted trade in such products as gold, timber, and palm oil, and threatened the security of the European forts. Local British, Dutch, and Danish authorities were all forced to come to terms with Asante, and in 1817 the African Company of Merchants signed a treaty of friendship that recognized the Asante' claim to sovereignty over large areas of the coast and its peoples. Some coastal people, primarily some of the Fante and the inhabitants of Accra however came to rely on British protection against Asante incursions, but the ability of the merchant companies to provide this security was limited. In 1821, the British Crown gave authority over British forts on the Gold Coast to Governor Charles MacCarthy, governor of Sierra Leone. His mandate was to create peace and to end the slave trade. He sought to do this by encouraging the coastal peoples to oppose Asante rule and by closing the great roads to the coast from the Asante. The result is sporadic warfare one in which MacCarthy was killed 1824. An Asante invasion of the coast in 1826 was defeated, nonetheless, by a combined force of British and local forces, including the Fantes and the people of

Accra. The British government decided to hand over the administration of the forts to British traders and grant them an annual subsidy of 4000 pounds. They were asked not to interfere with local politics. In 1829, a London committee of merchants chose Captain George Maclean to become president of a local council of merchants. Although his formal jurisdiction was limited, Maclean's achievements were substantial. He made a peace treaty with the Asante in 1831 and supervised the coastal people by holding regular court in Cape Coast where he punished those found guilty of disturbing the peace. Between 1830 and 1843 while Maclean was in charge of affairs on the Gold Coast, no confrontations occurred with the Asante, and the volume of trade reportedly increased threefold. The main exports from Ghana at this time were palm oil, gold, ivory, pepper and corn. The production of palm oil, coffee and corn greatly increased to the encouragement of British traders. Under his administration, several coastal tribes submitted voluntarily to British protection and he exercised a limited judicial power on the coast. Webster, Boahen & Tidy (1980, p. 53) assert that *the great extension of British power and influence was mainly the result of the work of George Maclean.* This is because he realised that unless peace and order were established in the Gold Coast, neither legitimate trade nor missionary activities would flourish. Therefore, he deliberately ignored the British government's instructions and actively interfered in local politics. Indeed, no sooner had he arrived than he began to negotiate with the Asante. These negotiations were successfully concluded and a peace treaty was signed by the Asante and the British and their allies in April 1831.

According to the terms of this treaty, the Asantehene recognised the independence of his former vassal states and agreed to refer all disputes between himself and the southern states to the British for peaceful settlement. He also agreed to deposit 600 ounces of gold in Cape Coast Castle, and to hand over two young men of the royal family to the British Government for six years as security that he would keep peace with the British and their allies. The allied states, for their part, undertook to keep the paths open and free to all persons engaged in lawful traffic, not to force them to trade in any particular market, and not to insult their former master. Finally, all parties to the treaty agreed to stop 'panyarring', that is, forcibly seizing debtors or relatives and imprisoning them or selling them. This treaty was a very clever piece of work, since it satisfied both principal parties.

The result is that the allied states at long last regained their independence, while the Asante gained direct access to the forts that they had been fighting for since the eighteenth century. Maclean also sought to maintain peace and order among the chiefs of the southern states, to stop human sacrifice, panyarring, attacks or raids on peaceful traders, and slave trading. He did this mainly by peaceful means, though he did not hesitate to use force when necessary.

The other method by which he made the presence of the British felt was in the administration of justice among the peoples. He attended the courts in person or sent a member of the council to watch the actual process of the trial and to see that justice was really done. Later on he also allowed the chiefs, as well as their subjects, to bring cases of all kinds to his court, and he tried the cases and imposed sentences of fines or imprisonment on the guilty. He also stationed magistrates in Anomabo and Accra. He also used the soldiers of the forts as police to see to it that order was maintained. The inability of this administration to completely prevent ships which took part in the slave trade from buying goods in the territory under British control was among the reasons for which the parliamentary committee recommended that the British government assume direct responsibility of the forts and negotiate treaties with the coastal chiefs. This was done in 1843 and Commander H. Worsley Hill was appointed first governor of the Gold Coast. Hill proceeded to define the conditions and responsibilities of his jurisdiction over the protected areas. He negotiated a special treaty that became known as the Bond of 1844. He signed the treaty on behalf of the British government, eight Fante chiefs of which eight came from Assin, Denkyira, Abora, Anomabo and Cape Coast signed on behalf of the people of Southern Ghana.

According to Webster, Boahen & Tidy (1980, pp. 54-156), the document contained three clauses. The first clause set down that the signatory chiefs recognised the power and jurisdiction that had been exercised in their states, and declared that 'the first objects of law are the protection of individuals and property'. The second clause stated that human sacrifice and 'other barbarous customs, such as panyarring, are abominable and contrary to law'. The third clause stated that murders, robberies and other crimes were to be tried before British judicial officers and the signatory chiefs, and that the customs of the country were to be 'moulded in accordance with the general principles of British law'.

Thus, the Bond recognised Maclean's former administration of justice and laid the legal foundation for subsequent British colonization of the coastal area. Additional coastal states as well as other states farther inland eventually signed the Bond, and British influence was accepted, strengthened, and expanded. Under the terms of the 1844 arrangement, the British were to protect the coastal areas. Thus, an informal protectorate came into being.

The other task that Hill and his successors tackled between 1843 and 1865 was that of promoting Western civilisation and trade. They had in view the construction of roads, hospitals and schools. Money was needed. In April 1852, some local chiefs and elders met at Cape Coast to consult with the governor on means of raising revenue. *The Poll Tax Ordinance* was passed by the Assembly of Chiefs, which met in Cape Coast. The bill was ratified by a similar body of chiefs that assembled in Accra. The ordinance imposed a tax of one shilling a year per head on every man, woman and child in the 'Protectorate'. With the governor's approval, the Council of Chiefs constituted itself as a legislative assembly. In approving its resolutions, the governor indicated that the Assembly of Chiefs should become a permanent feature of the protectorate's constitutional machinery, but the assembly was given no specific constitutional authority to pass laws or to levy taxes without the consent of the people. In 1872, British influence over the Gold Coast increased further when Britain purchased the Elmina Castle, the last of the Dutch forts along the coast. The Asante, who for years had considered the Dutch at Elmina as their allies, thereby lost their last trade outlet to the sea. To prevent this loss and to ensure that revenue received from that post continued, the Asante staged their last invasion of the coast in 1873. After early successes, they finally came up against well-trained British forces who compelled them to retreat. Later attempts to negotiate a settlement of the conflict with the British were rejected by the commander of the British forces, Major General Sir Garnet Wolseley. To settle the Asante problem permanently, in January 1874, the British invaded Asante with a sizable military force made up of 2,500 British soldiers and large numbers of local auxiliaries and occupation was imposed.

The subsequent peace treaty required the Asante to renounce any claim to many southern territories. The Asante also had to keep the road to Kumasi open to trade. From this point on, the power of the Asante steadily declined. The confederation slowly disintegrated as subject territories broke away and as protected regions defected to British rule. The warrior spirit of the nation was not entirely subdued. In 1896, the British dispatched another expedition that again occupied Kumasi and that forced the Asante Kingdom to become a protectorate of the British Crown. The position of the king was abolished and the incumbent was exiled. The core of the Asante federation accepted these terms reluctantly. In 1900, the Asante rebelled again but were defeated, and in 1902, the British proclaimed Asante a colony under the jurisdiction of the governor of the Gold Coast. In the meantime, the British became interested in the broad areas north of Asante, known generally as the Northern Territories. This interest was prompted primarily by the need to forestall the French and the Germans, who had been making rapid advances in the surrounding areas. British officials had first penetrated the area in the 1880s, and after 1896 protection was extended to northern areas whose trade with the coast had been controlled by the Asante. In 1898 and 1899, European colonial powers amicably demarcated the boundaries between the Northern Territories and the surrounding French and German colonies. In 1902 the Northern Territories were proclaimed a British protectorate. Like the Asante protectorate, the Northern Territories were placed under the authority of a resident commissioner who was responsible to the governor of the Gold Coast. The governor ruled both the Asante Kingdom and the Northern Territories by proclamations until 1946. With the north under British control, the three territories of the Gold Coast, namely the Colony (the coastal regions), the Asante Kingdom, and the Northern Territories, became, for all practical purposes, a single political unit, or crown colony, known as *"the dependency"* or simply as the Gold Coast. The borders of present-day Ghana were realized in May 1956 when the people of the Volta region, known as British Mandated Togoland, voted in a plebiscite to become part of modern Ghana.

Administration

An Executive Council and a Legislative Council assisted the governor. The Executive Council was a small advisory body of European officials that recommended laws and voted taxes subject to the governor's approval. The Legislative Council included the members of the Executive Council and unofficial members initially chosen from British commercial interests. After 1900, three chiefs and three other natives chosen from the Europeanized communities of Accra, Cape Coast, and Sekondi were added to the Legislative Council. The inclusion of natives from the Asante Kingdom and the Northern Territories did not take place until much later. Prior to 1925, the governor appointed all members of the Legislative Council and official members always outnumbered unofficial members. The structure of local government had its roots in traditional patterns of government. Village councils of chiefs and elders were almost exclusively responsible for the immediate needs of individual localities, including traditional law and order and the general welfare. However, the chiefs were responsible to a British official, a resident or district officer, who in turn was responsible to the central government. The resident officer also oversaw the operation of taxation, the treasury and courts, but always operated through the chief (Webster, Boahen & Tidy, 1980, p. 206). The chiefs, however, were to take instructions from their European supervisors. The plan, according to Lord Lugard, had the further advantage of civilizing the natives, because it exposed traditional rulers to the benefits of European political organization and values. This "civilizing" process notwithstanding, indirect rule had the ultimate advantage of guaranteeing the maintenance of law and order.

With indirect rule, the chiefs became responsible to the colonial authorities who supported them. In many respects, therefore, the power of each chief was greatly enhanced. Consequently, many chiefs and elders came to regard themselves as a ruling aristocracy. Government commissioners generally led their councils. In 1925, provincial councils of chiefs were established in all three territories of the colony, partly to give the chiefs a colony-wide function. This move was followed in 1927 by the promulgation of the *Native Administration Ordinance*, which replaced an 1883 arrangement that had placed chiefs in the Gold Coast Colony under British supervision. The purpose was to clarify and to regulate the powers and areas of jurisdiction of chiefs and councils. Councils were given specific responsibilities over disputed elections and the unseating of chiefs. The procedure for the election of chiefs was set forth and judicial powers were defined and delegated. Councils were entrusted with the role of defining customary law in their areas subject to the approval of the government. The provincial councils were empowered to become tribunals to decide matters of customary law when the dispute lay between chiefs in different hierarchies. In 1935, the Native Authorities Ordinance combined the central colonial government and the local authorities into a single governing system. New native authorities, appointed by the governor, were given wide powers of local government under the supervision of the central government's provincial commissioners, who ensured that their policies correspond with those of the central government. Until 1939, when the *Native Treasuries Ordinance* was passed there was no provision for local budgets (*Ghana: Colonial Administration*, data 1994-2004)

Socio-economic Policies

On the socio-economic front, communications were greatly improved. Tele-communication and postal services were initiated and the Sekondi-Tarkwa railroad was built to connect most of the important commercial centres of the south. By 1937, there were 9,700 kilometres of roads to facilitate the transport of minerals and other items. New crops were also introduced among them cocoa, which did not only become the first cash crop to the farmers of the interior, but also the core of the nation's economy in the 1920s when disease wiped out the trees of Brazil from where the seeds of the crop had been brought. The production of cocoa was mainly in the hands of the natives. The *Cocoa Marketing Board* was created in 1947 to assist farmers to step up their production and increase sales. By the end of that decade, the Gold Coast was exporting more than half of the world's cocoa supply. The colony's earnings increased further from the export of timber and gold. Gold, which initially brought Europeans to the Gold Coast, remained in the hands of the natives until the 1890s when modern modes of extracting minerals were introduced (*Ghana, Economic and Social Development Data* 1994-2004).

The government's role was confined mainly to the provision of such basic utilities as water, electricity, railways, roads, and postal services. Agriculture, commerce, banking, and industry were almost entirely in private hands, with foreign interests controlling the greater share in all of them except agriculture.

Educational Policies

Formal Education in Ghana dates back to the mercantile era preceding colonization. According to historians, European merchants and missionaries set up the first schools. This was already evident at the time of Maclean. He did not establish any schools himself for want of funds, but he gave the missionaries every encouragement.

By 1843, Andreas Riis, a Danish minister and missionary of the Basel Mission, had established a school at Akropong. Soon after that he opened others in Accra and Aburi. By 1843, twenty one missionary stations had been established in Ghana by the Wesleyans, and there were 360 children attending their schools. The Methodists expanded their missionary and educational activities during the second half of the nineteenth century. In view of their focus on education, they founded Mfantsipim School, which is the first secondary school in the Gold Coast, in 1876.

However, a formal state educational structure, modelled on the British system, was set up during the colonial period. The Achimota College was planned as an institution more thoroughly geared to produce Black Englishmen. It was designed to place native students in European hands at the kindergarten stage and keep them there until graduation at university level. Strong emphasis was placed on the mixing of staff and students at study, at work and at play. In other words, during the most impressionable and formative stage, natives were to be immersed in British culture and then emerge from the assimilating process, *becoming English in everything but colour.* After the Second World War, under pressure from the natives, money was poured into schools. Universities were founded and were tied as colleges to universities in the imperial country. They followed identical courses and in many cases insisted upon the same dress and even eating habits to produce Black Englishmen to take over the colonial structure built by the Europeans. This structure has gone through a series of reforms since Ghana gained independence in 1957. The Ministry of Education (MoE) with its implementing agencies, namely the Ghana Education Service (GES), the National Council on Tertiary Education (NCTE), and the Non-Formal Education Division (NFED) have been responsible for all levels of the educational system in Ghana from primary schools through to tertiary institutions. The MoE is responsible for formulating educational policy.

The educational policy formulated is implemented by the above-named implementing agencies. At the pre-tertiary level the GES is responsible; at the tertiary level, it is the responsibility of the NCTE; and at the non-formal level, the NFED is responsible. Today, education in Ghana aims to provide the following services: basic education for all; education and training for skills development with emphasis on science, technology and creativity, and higher education for the development of middle and top-level manpower requirements.

Missionary Activities

The presence of Christian missionaries on the coast of Ghana dates back to the arrival of the Portuguese in the 15th Century. However, it was the Basel/Presbyterian and Wesleyan/Methodist missionaries, who, in the 19th Century, laid the foundation for the Christian church in Ghana. Beginning their conversions in the coastal area and among the Akwapim, these missionaries established schools as *"nurseries of the church"* in which an educated African class was trained. However, much had not been accomplished when the British Governor, Maclean, began his term of office. During his term of office, the missionaries took advantage of the peace and order that existed and moved inland. At Akropong, they established a catechists' training college in 1848. In 1850, they established another one. From that time, the work of evangelization began to take root and to spread. (Webster, Boahen & Tidy, 1980, p. 55). Conversions were made and churches were built. Today the population of Ghana is made up of adherents of African Traditional Religion (ATR), Christianity, Islam as well as pockets of religions and sects of Eastern origin. Christianity, ATR and Islam are, however, the three dominant religions. The religious composition of Ghana in the first post-independence population census of 1960 was 41 percent Christians, 38 percent traditionalists, and 12 percent Muslims. The rest of the population (about 9 percent) had no religious affiliation.

Globalization

One other way by which Ghanaians come into contact with the West is through globalization. Some view the term globalization as a process that is beneficial to future world economic development and also inevitable and irreversible. Others regard it with hostility, even fear, believing that it increases inequality within and among nations, threatens employment and living standards and thwarts social progress. Economic *"globalization"* is seen as a historical process, the result of human innovation and technological progress. It refers to the increasing integration of economies around the world, particularly through trade and financial flows. The term sometimes also refers to the movement of people (labour) and knowledge (technology) across international borders. There are also broader cultural, political and environmental dimensions of globalization. Thus, globalization is the process of integration of the world community into a common system either economic or social. In other words, it is the intensification of worldwide social relation which link distant localities in such a way that local happenings are shaped by events occurring many miles away and vice versa. In theory, one can say that Ghana got access to more capital flows, technology, cheaper imports, and larger export markets as far as globalization is concerned. More generally, the country is exposed to knowledge about production methods, management techniques, export markets and economic policies. Available also is knowledge in outward oriented policies to promote efficiency through increased trade and investment, structural reform to encourage domestic competition, strong institutions and an effective government to foster good governance, education, training, and research and development to promote productivity, external debt management to ensure adequate resources for sustainable development, and the existence of seemingly unrestricted market access for all exports from other countries. The most striking aspect of this has been the integration of financial markets made possible by modern electronic communication. There is sharply increased private capital flow into the country. There is direct foreign investment and Ghanaians are all over the world looking for better employment opportunities.

Effects of the Encounter in General

Opinions are divided as regards the effect of the European contact with Ghana. While others concentrate on only the negative, others look at the positive only. For the purpose of our work we shall look at both sides of the coin briefly and show what impact the encounter has had on the individual.

Positive Effects

The first remarkable positive effect was the establishment of a greater degree of continuous peace and stability following the consolidation of the colonial system. The peace and order and positive encouragement provided by colonialism contributed to the spread of Christianity and Western education. The result is an increase in the number of the Westernized educated elite that now dominated the civil service of Ghana. We also see the introduction of the English language as a unifying factor for the numerous languages found in Ghana. The introduction of currency and with it banking activities and the tremendous expansion in the volume of trade between colonial Ghana and Europe in turn led to the total integration of the economy of Ghana into that of the world in general and into that of the capitalist economy of the colonial powers. The years after 1935 merely deepened this link and not even independence has fundamentally altered this relationship. Another significant development is the introduction of the modern, geographical, independent African state leading to nationalism which fosters a sense of identity and consciousness among the various classes or ethnic groups inhabiting each of the new states.

Although urbanisation was not unknown in pre-colonial Africa, it was the colonial period which saw the birth of completely new towns such as Takoradi. There was also an improvement in the quality of life, particularly for those living in the urban centres. This stems from the provision of social amenities such as hospitals, dispensaries, pipe borne water and sanitary facilities, as well as the increase in employment opportunities. A new judicial system and a new form of bureaucracy or civil service were also introduced and barbarous customs were abolished. Other improvements included water supply, drainage, hydroelectric projects, public buildings, town improvements, schools, hospitals, prisons, communication lines, and other services made available in theory to the individual.

Negative Effects

To start with, the whole idea of the European coming to Africa was not positive. We hear the story of a few people, who were by no means African, deciding what Africa and Africans should be like at a deal sealed by the signatures of the European potentate in Berlin in 1884. We witness the definition of African identities and nationalities within the borders not negotiated by Africans themselves. Communities which had previously not existed were established. With this deal, people who belonged to the same communities were separated and forced to bear loyalty to something not of their own making. In a setup like this, it is difficult to ascertain a policy that truly addresses the needs of people who are caught up in a multiplicity of identity, and a confusing state of being and belonging. For many, colonialism was a system designed for the exploitation of resources for the benefit of the colonizing nation. The colony was to be a source of raw natural resources, which were exported to the West for manufacturing. The finished products were then sent back to be sold to the colony at inflated rates. Although Lord Lugard, Governor-General of Nigeria from 1914-1919, pointed to the civilizing influence of indirect rule, critics of the policy argued that the element of popular participation was removed from the traditional political system. Despite the theoretical argument in favour of decentralization, indirect rule in practice caused chiefs to look to Accra (the capital) rather than to their people for all decisions. Indirect rule tended to preserve traditional forms and sources of power, however, it failed to provide meaningful opportunities for the growing number of educated young men anxious to find a niche in their country's development. Others were dissatisfied because there was not sufficient cooperation between the councils and the central government and because some felt that the local authorities were too dominated by the British district commissioners. Even by British standards, the chiefs were not given enough power to be effective instruments of indirect rule. Some Ghanaians believed that by increasing the power of the chiefs at the expense of local initiative, the reforms permitted the colonial government to avoid movement toward any form of popular participation in the colony's government. As far as the Christian missionary activities were concerned they were seen as a guise for European commercial activities.

They were the most ambitious ideological agents of the British Empire, bearing with them the fanatical zeal to reconstruct the native world in the name of God and Great Britain. This is evident in a speech at Oxford University in 1864 by British "Christian" missionary David Livingstone who is portrayed as the most dedicated missionary with a passionate vision for the "Dark Continent" (Africa). "Sending the Gospel to the heathens of Africa must include more than implied in the usual practice of a missionary namely, a man going about with a Bible under his arms. The promotion of commerce ought to be specially attended to as this, more than anything else, makes the heathen tribes depend on commercial intercourse among civilized nations. I go back to Africa to open a new path to commerce. Do you carry on the work I have started" (Tyehimba, 2004, n. p.)?

They were on a humanitarian "civilizing" mission, bringing salvation to the "primitive" tribes and "lost souls" but they were the fore-runners who paved the way for the colonial conquest.

The impact of colonialism in the cultural field is interesting. The Europeans who moved into Africa during this period, especially between 1900 and 1945, were generally filled with the spirit of cultural and racial superiority of the day. As a result, theirs was an attitude of condemning everything African, be it art, music, dance, names, religion, marriage, systems of inheritance, etc. Hence to be admitted into a church implied, for the African, not only baptism, but a complete change of name and renouncing the aforementioned cultural characteristics. For many, the least said about the economy the better. The system is seen to have been characterised by economic exploitation of the agricultural and mineral resources of colonies by the imperial powers. Trade was directed at the interests of the imperial power not the colonies. There was an almost total absence of modern manufacturing industrial development until the Second World War. There was the domination of the export trade by great Europeans at the expense of African farmers and traders (Webster, Boahen & Tidy (1980, p. 223). The introduction of the new mining methods saw the European mining companies and the colonial government accumulating much of the wealth. A policy of financing piecemeal development in the colonies out of the colonies' limited revenues did much harm to the economy as resources were depleted. The development of new forms of transport based especially on railways and motor vehicles were seen to have connected only areas where there were minerals to be transported. Considerable initiative by native farmers and traders in the continued development of export crops resulted in the negligence of other food products. This dissatisfaction is summarised by Webster, Boahen, & Tidy (1980, pp.55-56) as stated below.

There was hardly any modern manufacturing
industrial development in West Africa before

the Second World War. Industrialisation would compete with the industries of the imperial country and would upset the Colonial Pact. Moreover, local West African industries were allowed to die in competition with European manufactured goods. The development of railways allowed European cotton goods and iron tools to be sold in the interior much more cheaply than those of African manufacture. Generally, African craftsmen, especially weavers and blacksmiths, were hardest hit. Another idea in the Colonial Pact was that colonies must be financially self-supporting. Therefore, development projects such as harbours, railways and roads had to be built entirely out of local funds. Obviously, this limited the amount of development that could take place. Finance was not lacking in the imperial capitals, but it was invested in the British and French economies rather than in the colonies. The British treasury even deliberately held back development funds by a policy of creating reserve funds for the colonies. Reserve funds kept losing their real value through inflation.

So pathetic was the situation that at independence the economy of Ghana was largely dependent on the production and export of raw materials. Ghana also had a very poor infrastructure at the verge of independence, a poor feature indeed to serve as an economic base. It must be pointed out that colonial education was not designed to prepare Ghana for such a period of feverish economic development. Educated people did not possess the technical knowledge and skill to plan and carry through development programs. For the most part therefore, statesmen have had to rely on administrators trained for routine leisurely administration. The quality and orientation of the elite, which ran these programs, were also questionable. There was also the chronic lack of capital. The cost of paying loans and the salaries of the experts (mostly from the donor' countries), who executed the projects, were sufficient reasons to reject such an offer.

Impact of the Encounter on the Individual

There is no doubt that the encounter with the West has had great impact on the individual in the traditional set up. The impact is most felt in the political, social, cultural, economic and religious arena.

Political Sphere

Politically, the system drew boundaries of the new colonies for the convenience of the colonial masters. This often cut across ethnic and linguistic lines, often bringing together groups that were historically hostile (as in the case Ghana) to one another to live together as a nation. The individual from now on gets a new identity, becomes a citizen of a nation. To be successful within the new system, the individual would have to embrace and internalize the values of the colonizer. As a bearer of one basic traditional culture, the individual is expected to interact with fellow citizens who are themselves bearers of different basic traditional cultures. At the national or international level, he is confronted with a new way of life quite different from the traditional pattern, "*the western civilization*." Because the integration did not develop naturally and due to the fact that the western civilization did not go far enough to erase the traditional political system, the individual if forced to hold allegiance to traditional authorities and state authorities and when it is convenient to him, he shifts identity. Unfortunately, at the wake of independence there was assumption that the new independent countries would adopt and run the same sort of political system and government as their former colonial masters. This is evident in the kinds of constitutions which these states were given or made to adopt during the final stages of decolonization. Ghana was expected to operate what has come to be known as the ***Westminster parliamentary system of democracy*** characterized by the existence of two main parties which, would alternate between being in government and being in opposition, as well as a politically neutral civil service, armed forces and judiciary. This system of government operates on the principle of 'winner-take-all', which implies that the losing party has to content itself with being patient in the hope of winning in the next election. In a new nation carved out of different ethnic groups which were still fully conscious of their differences, and therefore with a shaky unity, and where people wanted a government that could bring rapid development, the system was bound to fail. Furthermore, Ghanaian politicians succeeded in making being in government a lucrative business. This resulted to a situation in which once a party came to power, whether by fair or foul means, it sought to keep it forever. The consequence of this is that parties which, found themselves out of government, and therefore in opposition, fearing exclusion from power for all time, sought every available means to gain power at the expense of the party in government. And so among other methods they would whip up ethnic or tribal sentiments, use unorthodox election methods usually leading to violence and rigging. They sometimes resorted to conspiracy, assassination and even instigated the armed forces to take over control of the state. But above all, the violence, which now characterized politics, began to make life unbearable for the individual. Corruption became endemic in the country. Military coups and dictatorship became obvious, soldiers now considered the logical alternative to politicians. This has been the case in Ghana after independence till the close of 1992. According to Oquaye (1980), the presence of the military in politics in Ghana could be traced to factors like lack of constant screening and self-analysis by political leaders, arrogance, deceit and giving of false hopes, suppression of the People, tribalism, political corruption, and refusal on the part of politicians to tolerate opposition or to accept the verdict of the electorate with good grace. It must be noted that both colonial and post-colonial governments created a distance between the government and the governed. This, in turn, provoked attitudes of unconcern and insensitivity to the affairs of the state on the part of the individual. Consequently, the general attitude of the individual was that it was possible to injure the state without injuring oneself, an attitude that opened the floodgates of bribery, corruption, carelessness about state property or state enterprises, and other unethical or antisocial acts. Traditional ideology which positively maintained that any injury done to the community as a whole directly injures the individual is abandoned by the individual. Thus, the traditional sentiments of personal commitment to the community was taken for granted by the individual.

Socio-economic Sphere

On the socio economic front we see a struggling individual. Prior to this time, the individual was driven by a sacred sense of responsibility towards his immediate families, lineage groups and societies. Now there exists greatly weakened lineage groups being replaced by nationalism. In this atmosphere many individual do not live on their ancestral lands anymore. In his new surroundings, he is not able to follow the traditions of his original culture. His way of life is no longer bound by the ethical and social norms of his original culture. He now holds aspirations of individual (as distinct from family) success. He is little inclined to sacrifice his own opportunities in favour of his siblings, or his children's opportunities in favour of his nephews and nieces. His decisions on important matters of his life are taken without calculation of the interests of his lineage group or kin group. In this environment, the very idea of a family becomes different. As Abraham (1992) observes, not only has the Western-style school with its new education and its different conception of the individual and his responsibility to others as well as its new attitude to nature become the order of the day but the street, whose gangs constitute the new age sets are the disparate systems by which the development of the youth must now be guided. He goes on to point out that under this condition social control is typically weakened, as the instruments and sanctions of traditional cultures are thwarted without equivalent substitutes. Punishment in its urban practice appears formal and cold, and its very purpose becomes a topic of discussion among different theories, whereas in the traditional society its purpose is always agreed. The new and complex set-up has not shown the same efficiency or success in establishing social coherence and unity as traditional cultures show where they have authority and dominance. However, the desirable life held up by modern mass media and the rhetoric of governments have convinced the individual that he ought to be dissatisfied with his state of life. It has then come to seem a matter of enlightenment and ambition to succumb to the lure of the cities and the so called first world countries. Unfortunately, the masses that move to urban areas, being mostly illiterate, also mostly lack the active skills and mental outlook relevant for acquiring the means to a meaningful life in an urban setting. This aggravates the problems of urban unemployment, and severely distorts the urban burden of welfare and social security. In this way, it creates within the urban areas, wildernesses of homelessness and impoverishment for the individual. But so powerful is the conviction of the comfort the new system is said to provide that, most individuals will risk every means possible to get to the cities or beyond. There have been many stories in the past and in recent times about people leaving their places of abode to seek greener pastures. For example, on 6th December, 2002, there was a newspaper report stating that two Ghanaian boys aged 12 and 14 had been found dead in the undercarriage well of an aeroplane at the Heathrow Airport. They were apparently trying to smuggle their way into Britain (The British Guardian, 2002). On the economic front, colonialism helped the spread of technology and promoted new agricultural and industrial methods of production. These new methods had an effect on social relations within communities, as it altered the way work was organised and resources were used. Traditional diversified agriculture was replaced by single-crop plantations. Banking, shipping and trading firms and companies were also introduced. There was also commercialization of land which led to the illegal sale of communal lands by unscrupulous family heads and to increasing litigation over land. The result is that the individual enters the cash economy in order to buy the food that they could no longer grow, as well as to pay their taxes. This often resulted in the break-up of the family, forcing men away to work in the new cities or in the mines, leaving the women at home in the villages to bear the burden of food production. As we have seen in the previous chapter, work would be possible only in groups.

Work would regularly be with other members of one's family or age set. Its purpose scarcely goes beyond the sustenance and well-being of the family, lineage group or community. In general, there would be no hiring of labour, each person carrying out family or social obligations as a matter of ethical imperatives. Now, labour is individual, and its competence, just like its rewards, is the individual's. Today, its driving force is economic necessity....... Hired farm hands who would have enjoyed rights in the land by virtue of their membership in their lineage groups, now work instead for wages, and have neither the inclination nor the power to continue the attitude of solicitude and respect towards the land, which the clan demands and fosters.

Dzobo (1992) in this regard, points out that, while the humanistic value orientation derives its origin from man's devotion to the ultimate or the infinite in the finite, market value orientation derives its source from devotion to man's economic and social interests and well-being, which are believed to be the chief ends of life. Instead of being seen as made up of creative humanities, society is now viewed as comprising incompatible individual socio-economic interests, divided into groups with opposing socio-economic interests. He observes a constant struggle by the individual in society to maintain and safeguard a privileged socio-economic interests and position. Life then becomes a struggle for existence and survival of the fittest, with the weak falling by the way. The most cherished value in this system is now power, economic power. Market-oriented values have become the prime and leading movers of both social and individual behaviour. He concludes that such main principles of a market-oriented life as competition and unbridled individualism have been introduced into the fabric of our society and various national governments either consciously or unconsciously have been attempting to build the nations upon it. Amidst the exigencies of urbanization and the increasing commercialization of agriculture, Wiredu (1992) observes that the ideology of mutual aid is losing some of its hold, and the spirit of neighbourhood solidarity, though by no means extinguished, is finding fewer sweeping avenues of expression.

Religious Sphere

One other area where the individual is also affected is religion. The Christian religion that was introduced by Europeans was embraced by the individual, as traditional religious practices were considered heathenish idolatry and devil-worship. Those converted were to change their names. Every African name has a meaning and significance. For example children in Ghana carry names of the day on which they were born. Parents may also name children after people who have done significant things in their lives. To keep the good name of such persons, parents honour them by naming a child after that person. However, the early Christians did not see it this way. For them these names were *heathen, primitive, uncivilized* and the individual who converts must acquire a new name, a European name. The individual saw himself, therefore, as transformed with a new name. The modern individual is born into a Christian family, attends a Christian school and becomes a Christian as a matter of course (rather than of conscious reflection) in the very process of his socialization. At the same time, the traditional religion with its concept is too present to the individual for him to overlook. The outcome is that he is partially brought up in both religions. According to Wiredu (1992), one is now asking himself how he can be both an African and a Christian. For him the answer that seems to be canvassed in the most influential circles of African Christians is that Africans can be Christians in good conscience only by Africanizing Christianity. So some Africans have even thought to Africanize Christ himself. It is common place to witness those artistic representations in which Jesus is depicted as a black man. But as far as one can see, forms of Africanizing the Christian religion (sometimes termed "*inculturation*") have been mainly concerned with the externals of the religion: *liturgy, forms of apparel, personnel,* etc. Wiredu (1992), like many other scholars, thinks that one should not underestimate the gains that have been made in the Africanizing of these aspects of the Christian religion. He cites an incident not long ago in which an African preacher in the Presbyterian Church in Ghana was disciplined for mounting the pulpit in his native attire. Now, even the Catholic Church permits songs in African rhythms and idiom, actually punctuated with drumming and dancing in the process of worship, a phenomenon which, a few years ago, would have seemed more inconceivable than that a donkey should transport itself through the hole of a needle. Today, no one who observed the subdued demeanour during worship in the more rigidly colonized modes can refuse to notice the contrasting spontaneity and joy with which many people participate in Christian worship electrified with traditional music. The present position is that in spite of much earnest and sincere nationalistic protestation, the individual Christian has hardly started to think of a critical reappraisal of Christian doctrine *vis-a-vis* his own native religion. The individual Christian continues to recognize the ancestors and numerous other spirits as part of the cosmological order. The action of the individual, for example, is seen to continue to affect the gods and spirits of the departed, while the support of family or "tribal" ancestors continue to ensure prosperity of the lineage and for that matter the individual. Veneration of departed ancestors remains a major obligation of the individual in the traditional system. The ancestors continue to be seen as the most immediate link with the spiritual world, and they are thought to be constantly near, observing every thought and action of the individual. Priests in the traditional religion undergo vigorous training in the arts of medicine, divination, and other related disciplines and are, therefore, consulted on a more regular basis by the individual for help under various circumstances. Because many diseases are believed to have spiritual causes, traditional priests sometimes act as doctors or herbalists. So that when medical treatment seems to be failing, it is common to see relatives moving patients to shrines for herbal treatment or undergoing both treatments simultaneously. Shrine visitation is strongest among the uneducated and in rural communities. This fact, however, does not necessarily suggest that the educated Ghanaian has totally abandoned tradition; some educated and mission-trained individuals do consult traditional oracles in times of crisis. It is also common to see Christians and Moslems visiting shrines after service. Sarpong (1998, pp.21-22) discussing Christianity and ATR writes:

> *Traditional religion can never be wiped out, in fact, in spite of all appearances, it has become part of our lives that our people whether educated or uneducated urban or rural at the level of spirituality continue to practice it...further more religious leaders like diviners, rainmakers, the priest, the herbalist continue to exert great influence on our people....now whether we like it or not Christians have one foot in that religion and one in Christianity.*

Wiredu (1992) observes that concepts such as" 'God', 'Spirit', 'Soul', 'Salvation', 'the Mystical', 'the Supernatural', 'Creation', 'Omnipotence'" have made their way deep into the scheme of concepts and continue be used as if their intelligibility or internal coherence in all human language and thought can be taken for granted.

Intellectual Sphere

Intellectually, the individual now thinks in the national languages in which he is educated. As far as concepts such as "'Being', 'Existence', 'Entity', 'Nothingness',

'Substance', 'Quality', 'Truth', 'Fact', 'Reality', 'Matter', 'Body', 'Mind', 'Person', 'Space', 'Punishment', 'Free Will', etc. are concerned, most individuals might just as well be called Europeans. Yet Wiredu (1992) sees very radical differences between the manner in which the matters involved are conceived in our indigenous languages and thought, on the one hand, and in the metropolitan languages and thought, on the other. The individual becomes extremely affected by what many have referred to as *colonial mentality*. This, Wiredu (1992) explains as the mentality which makes a formerly colonized person over-value foreign things coming from his erstwhile colonial master. He explains that 'Things' here is to be interpreted widely to include not only material objects but also modes of thought and behaviour. We to see an individual who carries within himself a base of traditional culture upon which profoundly wrenching demands are made on the one hand and on the other hand an individual in whom consciousness of elements of the colonial mentality have been so deeply ingrained that even the fiercest denunciation of colonialism or the most fundamentalist affirmation of indigenous culture is no more possible. From the foregoing analyses, we observe the individual beset by an identity crisis that seems rather difficult to overcome. This crisis haunts him on the socio-political and ideo-psychological levels. It haunts him in the clothes he wears, the food he eats, the language he speaks, the way he worships, the way he rules or is ruled, the way he acts or reacts. *Ideologically, he is torn between Western concepts and traditional concepts.* With regard to belief, he is expected to be converted to one or several of the options and loyally conform to their demands. No wonder then he never quite seems to attain complete "conversion", but rather seems to habitually "depart from orthodoxy" preferring on many occasions to follow the ways of his fathers.

Conclusion

From the foregoing analyses, we have seen that the Ghanaian encounter with the Western system of thought was gradual. It began with normal trade in traditional goods which gave way to slave trade and return to normal trade or legitimate trade as it was called. The importance of these is seen in the fact that some Ghanaians became trade partners with the Europeans. The obvious result is that other ways of trading differed from the one known before the encounter was introduced. To ensure free trade and peace, the tribes accepted the British protection and with that Western system of governance, way of life, and education were introduced. Western religion was also introduced, symbolically giving new identity to those who embraced it by the new names they acquired. With the attainment of independence came a new identity because the individual now became the citizen of a nation; he has been baptised with a new name so he is a Christian, educated in the Western line of thought so he sees himself enlightened or civilised. The traditional societies were now irreversibly penetrated by a new brand of Western thought system dominated by colonial powers. This thought system altered the force and direction of the host cultures, altered social relations and the rationale underlying the organization of traditional societies. New ways of doing things and new reasons for doing them were introduced. Cultures, which before were highly territorial, were brought within common territories. In a word, these encounters changed in many different ways at one and the same time relations between individuals and relations with the environment. We observe rapid interactions with the consequent intermingling of cultures, through their mutual acknowledgement and the mutual influences of their politics, economics, religion, literature, art and education to mention but a few. Because the transition was unnatural, rapid and incomplete the individual is in a kind of crisis, torn between two worlds as pointed out above. The crisis haunts him on the social, political and ideological psychological fronts. It affects him in the clothes he wears, the food he eats, the language he speaks, the way he worships, the way he rules or is ruled, the way he acts or reacts. Ideologically, he is torn between Western concepts and traditional concepts. With regard to belief, he is expected to be converted to one or several of the options and loyally conform to their demands. Our concern in the next chapter will be to look at what efforts are being made to give some kind of meaning to the individual in the society in which he finds himself today.

CHAPTER FIVE

THE INDIVIDUAL IN THE GHANAIAN SOCIETY TODAY

Introduction

After we have informed ourselves about the encounter with the Western thought system and looked at some of its impact on the individual we shall now look at some reactions to this situation and what efforts are being made to help the individual have a clear cut way of life. Before trying a definition, the state of the country will be looked at. This will enable us to see that the individual lives in a society quite different from the society before the encounter.

Crises in Identity

As we saw at the close of the fourth chapter, the individual is in a kind of crises. Politically, he holds allegiance to the state and to the traditional authorities. On the socio-economic front, he is torn between working to feed the extended family and concentrating on his nuclear family. On the religious front, he has accepted religions such as the Christianity, Islam, etc. that hitherto were not practiced in his culture, but he cannot let go his former beliefs. Intellectually, his education is modelled on the Western system of thought, but he is without adequate facilities that reach a Western standard of education. The crises haunt him on the social, political and ideological and psychological fronts to mention but a few. They haunt him in the clothes he wears, the food he eats, the language he speaks, the way he worships, the way he rules or is ruled, and the way he acts or reacts to situations. Ideologically, he is torn between Western concepts and traditional concepts. In terms of belief, he is expected to be converted to one or more belief systems and loyally conform to their demands. The main cause of this identity crises, according to Wiredu (1992, p.62), could be reduced to the fact that the dominance of this colonial mentality was incomplete. Of course, had it been absolute, there could not have been so much sense of identity crisis. The obvious fact of this consciousness in Ghana shows that indigenous modes of thought and action were not totally eclipsed by colonialism. He further observes that a circumstance that has limited the psychological penetration of colonialism is that the colonialists did not trouble themselves much to 'educate' the populations in the rural interior of lands they colonized. Consequently, the people of these lands still retain large parts of their indigenous world outlook. This has resulted in the fact that even the educated individual has never been completely cut off from his culture. At the school, some colonial teachers and missionaries, who thought the colonized did not have their own history and culture, made their students to learn their history and culture. For example, the educated Ghanaian had to adopt the English language because the colonial master considered his local language(s) to be too simple. Furthermore, he was thought to be incapable of poetry and without abstract thought. European medical and social practices were also considered to be superior to those of the colonized people. For example, the colonialists frowned upon the colonized people's respect for the wisdom of their ancestors. The successful individual felt great pressure to devalue or forget his heritage in favour of exported Western values that were supposedly superior. In fact, anything Western was to be considered superior. It is, however, interesting to note that the system was obviously built upon a sense of the superiority of the White race. Consequently, race mixing was naturally frowned upon. Thus, the educated individual tended to consort with others of his own class, and as a result of the fact that they had internalized colonialist values, they tended to look down upon their non-elite brethren. They spoke the colonialist language among themselves, and came to cling fiercely to their positions of relative privilege. To a greater or lesser degree, they suppressed their cultural identity and became alienated from it (Oquaye, 1980, p. 3). Outlining reasons for which colonialism was able to make such deep inroads in the psychology of the individual, Wiredu points out that the colonialists came with superior science and technology, as he writes:

In many places they brought literacy where there was none. In these respects the gap was decisive; which, in the particular case of technology, is why the invaders were able to subjugate our ancestors in the first place. It was, of course, no mistake on the part of our ancestors to recognize this superiority in science and technology as manifested in the techniques and products of the colonialists. But the question is not so clear-cut when it comes to the religion, law, state-craft, mores, language, etc., which came as part of the colonial package. Having accepted one part, our people were led to transfer their approval to the other parts of the package. It was principally through the teachings of the missionaries who came along with the colonialists to `civilize' us and save our souls. Their campaign was only too successful (Encyclopaedia Britannica, 1994 -2001).

Reactions

As a result of the above, concerns have been raised as to how best these crises could be resolved. Whiles governments look to Western methods to equip the people with the means of transforming their societies into effective and prosperous modern nations (*Ghana, Country Profile ECONOMY*; op cit, a *Country Study*), others advocate a return to the roots. Nigeria's Mbonu Ojike thinks the best way out is to *"boycott all boycottables,"* meaning a severance of all links and a renunciation of anything that is not "home-made" to Africa. That would be like winding the clock backwards. Leopold Senghor would have intermarriage between the African values and the "civilized values," physically through a process of *miscegenation*, and ideologically through a process of assimilation. Paulin Hountondji thinks that it is not sufficient to study African cultures; they must be lived and practiced and, where necessary, transformed (Mbonu Ojike & Leopold Senghor as cited in Onyeocha, 1997, n. p.; Abraham, 1992, p.30). As to how this could be achieved, he thinks the best way is to adopt Western science (*World Factbook*, n. d.). Asante (1980) advocates the need for the individual to be re-located historically, economically, socially, politically, and philosophically. This is because for him, for far too long the individual has held up the margins of the European world and has been victimized by the illusion that he is working in his own best interests, when, in fact, he has become the chief apologist for Europe. Afrocentricity for him is necessary because it seeks to re-locate the individual as an agent in human history, an effort that will eliminate the illusion of the fringes, thus destroying the notion of being objects in the Western project of domination. Afrocentrists argue for pluralism in philosophical views without hierarchy. All cultural centers must be respected. Consequently, it becomes necessary to examine all data from the standpoint of Africans as subjects, human agents rather than as objects in a European frame of reference. The theorists contend that human beings cannot dispossess themselves of culture. The individual is either participating in his own historical culture or that of some other group. He acknowledges the fact that one can, of course, choose to opt out for one's own cultural heritage and appropriate that of some other people but this is rarely the case, however, with Europeans. They do not choose to become Indians or Chinese or Africans. His question is: why should the African do that? (Encyclopaedia Britannica, 1994-2001).

While Nkrumah (1964) calls for *Consciencism*, Ngũgĩ wa Thiong'o and Kwesi Wiredu call for a work to decolonize the mind by decolonization (Encyclopaedia Britannica, 1994-2001). Wiredu (1992, p.67) means divesting African philosophical thinking of all undue influences emanating from our colonial past. The crucial word in this formulation is "undue". He agrees that it would not be rational to try to reject everything of a colonial ancestry, because a thought or a mode of inquiry spearheaded by our erstwhile colonizers may be valid or in some way beneficial to humankind. Yet, there are reasons for adopting a doubly critical stance toward the problems and theories of Western philosophy particularly toward the categories of thought embedded therein. He thinks that colonialism was not only a political imposition, but also a cultural one. Gravely affected, or even perhaps infected, were religions and systems of education. Education was delivered in the medium of one foreign language or another. But a language, most assuredly, is not conceptually neutral; syntax and vocabulary are apt to suggest definite modes of conceptualization. For him, the individual who has learned philosophy in English, for example, has most likely become conceptually westernized to a large extent not by choice but by the force of historical circumstances. To that same extent he may have become de-Africanized. It does not matter if the philosophy learned was African philosophy. If that philosophy was academically formulated in English and articulated therein, the message was already substantially westernized, unless there was a conscious effort toward cross-cultural filtration. He sees colonized minds as minds that think about and expound their own culture in terms of categories of a colonial origin without any qualms as to any possible conceptual incongruities. Moreover, ordinary common sense dictates that one should not discard what is one's own in favour of what has come from abroad for no reason at all. Decolonization, then, has nothing to do with the attitude which implies that Ghanaians should steer clear of those philosophical disciplines that have at this particular point in human history received their greatest development in the West. He advocates for the decolonization of those elements of culture that play significant roles in the constitution of meanings in the various African world views. Of these, language stands pre-eminent. This has meant that wittingly or, most likely unwittingly, African conceptions of the relevant subjects have been assimilated to Western ones. In another development, he also called for the domestication in certain disciplines. By domestication he does not mean the mindless copying of conclusions arrived at somewhere else but taking up broad intellectual concerns relating to certain subject matters.

Wiredu further explains that colonialism is not necessarily racist in the sense in which the concept involves claims of racial superiority on the part of the colonizer; but it frequently goes with some sense of superiority. The racism associated with it was not just a state of mind, but an active program which sought to change the supposedly inferior way of life of the individual in Ghana in order to conform to European models in some important areas of human experience, such as education, religion, economics, politics, etc. He, therefore, sees it as natural that the anti-colonial struggle should take the form of both a cultural and a political nationalism, a political nationalism aimed at regaining national independence and then building viable modern states and a cultural nationalism aimed to restore to the individual his confidence in his own culture. He thinks that cultural nationalism was particularly urgent as colonial racism had succeeded in alienating many individuals from their own culture. He explains that ' anti-colonial nationalism stems from the fact that we became what we are now, not of our own free will, but rather through a colonial imposition. He distinguishes three types of cultural change; they include change which is deliberate and self-initiated and which substitutes something original for an old cultural element; change which is deliberate and self-initiated, but which involves foreign substitutes; change which is neither self-initiated nor original in its replacements. From the point of view of the problem of identity he asserts that the first type is the least, and the third the most problematic. It is better to accept change by one's own decision than through foreign pressures. It is better because it displays a greater degree of free will, and free will is a basic human ideal. It is better, moreover, from the point of view of the present discussion because it does not necessarily generate an identity crisis. If you change aspects of your culture and adopt in their place new ones of your own devising, then, even when there is trouble, any malaise would not be owing to a sense of compromised identity. Africans seem at some stages to have been of the third type (*World Fact Book*, n. d.).

Even though the aspect of colour does not seem to provide the ultimate answer to the question of any identity, it is, however, noteworthy that most of the attempts at identifying the individual, even by Africans themselves, have never quite succeeded in getting away from the question of colour. One possible explanation is the fact that the human mind often tends to work within established categories such that opinions earlier held tend to influence subsequent views. The individual Ghanaian among Westerners thinks he does not pass simply like any other person, but always is considered minutely with some uncanny curiosity. Sharing his personal experience that seem to reflect the lot of Africans in the Western world, Frantz Fanon thinks that, *the schema of his normal body experience had dissolved, attacked at several points, gave way and was replaced by a schema that was racial and epidemic* (Encyclopaedia Britannica, 1994-2001). In the train, he is responsible at one and the same time for *his body*, *his race*, and for *his ancestors*. He looks at himself objectively, discovered his blackness, his ethnic characteristics and he understands all that is being held against him; cultural backwardness, fetishism, slavery, cannibalism. All he wants, however, is to be a human being, nothing more than a human being. As a result of this kind of situation, some want to change their colour, liberate themselves from the burdensome memory represented in the skin. Others want to seek their salvation in the acquisition of the African heritage in the new-fangled spirit of Pan-Africanism. Nigeria's Nnamdi Azikiwe wisely warns against the danger of a too-narrow definition of the individual along racial lines (Onyeocha, 1997, n. p.). To do so would amount to parochialism, and chauvinism. It builds a wall between "Us" and "Them". In daily life, one who is conscious of being or having something peculiar is likely to be eternally recluse, not relaxed, and always on his guard. Being black does not have to divide the African away from the rest of humanity. If anything, it should be a perspective or channel for joining the wider family of humankind. Nigeria's late Prime Minister, Tafawa Balewa, promptly distances himself from any such activity. He states ***I do not believe in what some people call the African personality. There is no such thing as African personality. Africans belong to the human race and a talk of African personality betrays an inferiority complex*** (Onyeocha, 1997, n. p.).

Nkrumah (1964) explains the principle of equal opportunity and the consideration of man as an end rather than a means. According to him, Philosophical Consciencism forms the theoretical basis for an ideology whose aim shall be to contain the individual's experience of Islamic and Euro-Christian presence as well as the experience of traditional African society, and, by conception, employ them for the harmonious growth and development of that society. He recognizes that the individual is and does possess something of value that could be enriched by contact with the Euro-Christian and Islamic values. On the ideological level therefore he envisages a kind of federated approach whereby the individual can rescue for himself what is best in Christianity, Islam and the traditional values. Nkrumah did not want to arbitrarily deny the individual the gift of analytical and discursive reason. At the inauguration of the University of Ghana, in November 1961, he had never had any doubt about the intellectual capacity of the African (Onyeocha, 1997, n. p.). For him, acculturation in Ghana will be the means for interweaving the present diversity of cultures into a coherent whole from which can be derived the ends and the means of the general flourishing of society. The anticipated result of the acculturation will be the re-invigoration of Ghanaian cultures, enriched by the colonial, the Islamic, and the Christian experience in a manner and to an extent which are beneficial to the individual in his current environment.

Defining the Individual in Ghana Today

With the stage marked by dogmatism, inflexibility, and general combativeness, which cumulatively were the assertion of a separate identity, there is a possibility to assess our conception of the individual. With the specification of a cloak and a persona, through which thoughtful spokesmen for their African compatriots sought to be grasped, a unique reaction, entirely similar to the efforts of various European spokesmen, in particular, certain German thinkers, to describe and thereby constitute the "*Volkgeist*" or '*Spirit of the people'* in reaction to the eighteenth century domination of Europe by French culture, at its end, there is room for us to rethink the individual (Mackenzi, n. d.). As a Ghanaian proverb puts it *the best way out of sleep is to wake up, especially if the sleep is time-wasting.* No one can be praised forever for failing to get out of a time wasting sleep no matter the circumstances that led to the inactivity. The individual today has many avenues for self-realization but his embattled situation must be recognized as such by him if he is to make use of the opportunities which present themselves to him. To get at this individual, the contribution of the West is a useful and helpful supplement, while the individual self-affirmation leads the way. Crucial to the question of personality development is contentment with what one is or has, while not giving up on what one should be. To get a better understanding of what the individual is, we shall look at the environment in which he finds himself today.

A Wink at Ghana

A quick look at Ghana today will reveal that most individuals are further away from the traditional thought system than they are nearer to the Western thought system.

At all levels in government and in public life, efforts are being made to play down tribal differences, a policy that has been helped by the adoption of English as the official used in government, large-scale businesses, national media, and schools beyond primary level.

At independence in 1957, the Westminster parliamentary democracy that was introduced with Dr. Kwame Nkrumah as the President was alien to African thought. It was a democracy imported from the colonial master. At the beginning of his rule, Nkrumah was popular in Ghana and much admired by African nationalist leaders. This was because "...the President called for all efforts to be concentrated upon building a first class nation. He condemned the evils of using one's office for personal gain or amassing wealth, rumour-mongering, using names of persons in prominent positions to collect money for oneself, patronising others for immoral favours, nepotism, etc. Those evils, he declared will be crushed in the most ruthless manner... (they) will be uprooted no matter whose ox is gored" (Khudadjie, 1995, p.5). In spite of these laudable ideals, the young Westminster democracy could not be sustained. Barely nine years after its introduction, some military officers and police officers, led by Colonel Emmanuel Kwasi Kotoka, staged a bloody coup d'état on 24th February, 1966, while Nkrumah was abroad. The government of the Convention People's Party (CPP) under Nkrumah was noted for its corrupt administration, massive foreign debts, and declining living standards. Initially, he disillusioned many supporters when he fostered his own personal cult, assuming the honorific title of *Osagyefo* (*he who is successful at war*). In Ghana, he adopted draconian measures to concentrate power in his hands and to crush any opposition. Isolated from his people, he listened only to self-seeking sycophants and allowed the CPP to become entwined in a web of corruption and intrigue. In 1958, he removed the obligation to consult regional assemblies on constitutional changes and in 1960 made Ghana a republic with himself as President. In 1964, he finally eliminated any legal opposition by making Ghana a single-party socialist state. Internationally, he moved closer to the communist world, while maintaining his own version of socialism and seeking Western financial aid in his attempt to break Ghana's dependence on cocoa. The economy was overspent and Ghana accumulated huge debts. Commenting on Nkrumah's government, Oquaye (1980) observes that academic freedom, freedom of the press, freedom of speech, and freedom of association, were strangled. Judges were arbitrarily dismissed, the State was declared non-partisan and members of parliament were subsequently handpicked by Nkrumah. Thereafter, parliament was reduced to a mere rubber-stamp body. By the time Nkrumah was overthrown, it was crystal clear that all avenues to constitutional change had been blocked and the right of the people to choose their own leaders through free and fair elections had become a nightmare. A large section of Ghanaians, who were faced with the harsh political, social, and economic problems, were happy that Dr. Nkrumah's regime had been ousted. Dr. Nkrumah went into exile in Guinea, where he died (The Guardian, 06 Dec 2002). The coup plotters took over power and formed The *National Liberation Council* (NLC), which was led by Lieutenant General Joseph

Ankrah. The leadership of the new government failed to redeem a promise to restore parliamentary democracy as expected resulting in a change in leadership in the same government. In spite of problems that the NLC had, a cardinal and often-admired achievement that the government chalked was that it was able to hand over the government to civilians without much delay after free and fair elections. A constituent assembly produced a constitution for a second republic, and general elections, which were won by the Progress Party (PP), were held in August 1969. This ushered in the Ghana's Second Republic that was inaugurated on 1st October, 1969. The newly-formed civilian regime, which was led by Dr. Kofi Abrefa Busia could not make an economic turnaround. During the Second Republic …"if public morality did not deteriorate, it certainly, it certainly did not show any significant improvement either… In his assessment of the Busia regime, Le Vine came to the conclusion that it was guilty of the same kinds of evil, that the Nkrumah regime was guilty of" (Khudadjie, 1995, p. 29). In January 1972, some army officers dissatisfied with political ineptitude, arrogance, intolerance of criticism, and enthusiasm for the plusher rewards of office (Khudadjie, 1995), staged a second coup d´état and took over the reins of government. The new government called the *National Redemption Council* (NRC) was chaired by the then Colonel Ignatius Acheampong. In 1975, the NRC was reorganized to include some civilians, but ultimate power was given to the *Supreme Military Council*. In 1978, Acheampong, who had elevated himself to the rank of a General, proposed a "Union Government, whose leadership was to be made up of military men and civilians sharing power. The acceptance of that proposal would have meant the placement of a ban on all political parties. A national referendum held to approve the proposal served mainly to show the unpopularity of the NRC. There was a palace coup, which placed Lieutenant General Frederick W.K. Akuffo in charge of affairs. In 1979, young officers and non-commissioned officers led by Flight Lieutenant Jerry John Rawlings of the Ghana Air Force overthrew the Government of Acheampong. In the heat of what the new military junta termed a revolution, many Ghanaians lost a lot of property, while others lost their lives. Among those, who lost their lives, were General Acheampong and some of his close allies in government. In fact, General Acheampong and two other former Heads of State in the persons of Brigadier A. A. Afrifa and Lt. Gen. F.W. K. Akuffo as well as five those high-ranking officers in previous Governments were executed by firing squad. A return to parliamentary democracy proceeded the same year, as planned by the Rawlings led Armed Forces Revolutionary Council (AFRC), which had conducted itself creditably during its four months rule leaving " an example of accountability, probity, a sense of duty and service, simplicity, concern for the nation" (Khudadjie, 1995, p. 34). After winning the elections held, the People's National Party (PNP) put forward its flag bearer, Dr. Hilla Limann, to serve as President. This marked the birth of the Third Republic in September 1979. Like governments before it, the Government of the PNP pledged to serve the interest of the people, however, the radical improvements in the political and economic life of

Ghana looked for by Rawlings and his colleagues were slow. On 31st December, 1981, Rawlings led a military coup again and became the Head of State and Chairman of the *Provisional National Defence Council* (PNDC). Like its predecessor, the AFRC, the PNDC was "…committed to the moral transformation of the Ghanaian society, raising the standard of living, and establishing such liberties and rights as would make the Ghanaian live a life of liberty" (Khudadjie, 1995, p. 35). Right from the onset, the Government seemed to be doing well in their lifestyle and probity. However, this creditable performance was not sustained. "Now and then, some high state official or other member of an organ of the revolution was found guilty of an impropriety and was convicted" (Khudadjie, 1995, p. 35). Furthermore, the Government clamped down on free discussion and expression of opinion, "fostering what came to be known as the culture of silence" (Khudajie, 1995, p. 37). In the face of these difficulties, the regime's g\"glory" as the personification of social justice and moral probity faded. Even the regime's early admirers became completely disillusioned and disenchanted (Khudadjie, 1995). With a lot of pressure at home, due to the political, social, and economic problems coupled with pressure from the international community, the Government had no other choice than to introduce genuine participatory democratic processes. In 1992, a new constitution established a multiparty democratic system. The PNDC adopted a new name – National Democratic Congress (NDC). The new party won the general elections and Jerry John Rawlings became the first President of Ghana's fourth Republic. Since 1992 Ghana has been practicing the new presidential democracy and the country continues to make efforts for the system to work, thereby making the individual enjoy a stable government in which he can develop himself. The Constitution has put in place the roles and responsibilities for the three arms of government, namely the Executive, the Legislator, and the Judiciary. It ensures a government elected by universal suffrage and a legal system based on Ghanaian common law and customary (traditional) law. The country's court hierarchy consists of the Supreme Court, i.e. the highest court, the Court of Appeal, and High Court. Beneath these bodies are district, traditional, and local courts. Since independence, fervently devoted to the ideals of nonalignment and Pan-Africanism, both of which are closely identified with the first President, Kwame Nkrumah, Ghana consistently favours international and regional political and economic cooperation. She is an active member of the United Nations and African Union (AU), which was formerly called the Organization of African Unity (OAU).

The Economy

Today, Ghana's economy can be said to be a mixture of private and public enterprise. Gold, timber, and cocoa production are the major sources of foreign exchange. These products, at independence, made the country relatively prosperous. As a result of weak commodity demand, outmoded equipment, overvalued currency, smuggling, and huge foreign debts incurred after mid-1960s, the economy stagnated. Since 1983, the country's *Economic Recovery Program*, i.e. a structural adjustment program, has resulted in new investment and rising exports of cocoa, gold, and timber, but high foreign debts has prevented improvement in the standard of living. Today the domestic economy continues to revolve around subsistence agriculture, which employs 60% of the work force, mainly small landholders. The labour force, according to the year 2000 estimate, was 9 million. Ghana remains heavily dependent on international financial and technical assistance.

Education

Ghana has one of the best educational systems and one of the highest adult literacy rates in tropical Africa, but the cost (the amount of money) involved in education is high. The first cycle is free and compulsory; for the first three years education is in the predominant local language, with provision for education in at least one other Ghanaian language and English, the latter being the language of instruction from the fourth year of the primary cycle. There are numerous educational institutions throughout the country. These include crèches, nurseries, kindergartens, primary schools, junior high schools, senior high schools, commercial schools, technical schools, vocational schools, teachers' training colleges, nurses' training colleges, seminaries, agricultural training colleges, colleges of art and film, polytechnics and universities. The teachers' training colleges (now colleges of education) and nurses' training colleges used to be certificate awarding educational institutions, but they have been given accreditation to award diplomas. All the polytechnics used to award certificates and diplomas, and higher national diplomas, but most of them, with the exception of Wa Polytechnic and Bolgatanga Polytechnic, whose statuses have not changed, are now technical universities. These technical universities are Accra Technical University, Cape Coast Technical University, Takoradi Technical University, Koforidua Technical University, Kumasi Technical University, Sunyani Technical University, Ho Technical University, and Tamale Technical University. Apart from these technical universities, the country boasts of nine (9) other public universities, namely the University of Ghana (UG) at Legon-Accra, the University of Cape Coast (UCC), the Kwame Nkrumah University of Science and Technology (KNUST), which was formerly known as the University of Science and Technology at Kumasi, the University of Development Studies (UDS) at Tamale, the University of Education (UEW) at Winneba, the University of Health and Allied Sciences (UHAS) at Ho, the University of Professional Studies Accra (UPSA) at Madina-Accra, the University of Energy and Natural Resources (UENR) at Sunyani and the University of Mines and Technology (UMaT) at Tarkwa . In addition to the above, there are a number of private universities and specialized tertiary institutions in the country. The enrolment in all schools, especially in secondary, now called senior high schools, has soared dramatically since Ghana achieved self-government. But young children of school-going age could often be found during the day performing menial tasks in the agricultural sector or in the markets. The number of available places in second and third cycle institutions, especially the universities, however, is still far short of the demand from qualified applicants. Education for all remains an unrealized goal, but most children have access to primary and junior high schools. Vernacular and English are the languages of instruction at the primary level. All students pay textbook fees. Adult literacy rate reportedly stands at about 40 percent. In 1987, the system of six years of education at the primary level, four years at the middle school level, seven years at the secondary school level and four years at the university (6- 4-7-4) was changed to six years for primary schools, three years for junior high schools, three years for senior high schools, and four years for university education. Another important change was a reduction in the number of subjects. It is interesting to note that the duration of three years at the junior high school level was changed to four years from 2007-2009 during the New Patriotic Party Government led by President John Agyekum Kufuor. However, the duration was again changed to three years, when the National Democratic Party (NDC) won elections and President John Evans Atta Mills led its Government.

Justifying the need for the reforms, Assimeng (1999) pointed out that a very close examination of the performance of the economy in Ghana readily reveals that the nation perhaps has people who are overqualified, considering the nature of jobs that such qualified labour is expected to perform. Equally, a very large body of educated and semi-educated persons also exists, some of whom can hardly spell their own names properly. As it is such people cannot be relied upon to support high level administrative personnel in an increasingly complex economic organization activity. He goes on to explain that a major difficulty facing the performance of the economy appears to be a shortage of qualified and reliable middle level personnel. These middle level qualified and reliable personnel are required to serve as stenographer secretaries, laboratory technicians, X-ray technicians, physician assistants, agricultural mechanization and extension officers, first line family child welfare counsellors, computer data or entry processing clerks, etc. He explains further that university graduates, especially those in the disciplines of the humanities and the social sciences, with the exception of perhaps of those who are studying Economics, Management, Accounting, and Human Resource Management, are increasingly pouring out of the university system, only to face uncertain futures. There is, to put it bluntly, unemployment among such graduates. He thinks that graduates in law, medicine, business administration and accounting, surveying and architecture stand a better chance for now. But, world commerce seems to advocate hope for physician assistants, clerks, accounting assistants, and computer middle level functionaries, than their highly qualified but apparently less adaptable colleagues.

Health

Ghana has a reasonably good health service in the sub-region. All regional capitals and most districts and municipalities have hospitals and clinics. There are six teaching hospitals, namely the Korle-Bu Teaching Hospital, the University of Ghana Teaching Hospital, and the 37 Military Teaching Hospital all in Accra as well as the Okomfo Anokye Teaching Hospital in Kumasi, the Tamale Teaching Hospital, and the Cape Coast Teaching Hospital. All these health institutions have facilities for treating special cases. Additionally, a number of religious organizations and private medical practitioners operate hospitals and clinics all over the country. Herbal medicine and psychic healing are also generally practiced, and there is a special government Herbal Medicine Hospital and Research Centre at Akwapim-Mampong in the Eastern Region. The infant mortality rate has shown a steady decline, especially in urban areas, as a result of improved health care facilities and dietary habits; it is among the lowest in Western Africa but remains high by world standards (Ghana: a Country Study/Federal Research Division of the Library of Congress, 1995). A large number of infectious diseases endemic to tropics, including cholera, typhoid, tuberculosis, anthrax, yellow fever, hepatitis, trachoma, and malaria, guinea worm, dysentery, and onchocerciasis, to mention but a few, continue to give problems to the health authorities.

Religions

Theoretically, there is freedom of religion in Ghana. The population of Ghana, as pointed out above, comprises mainly practitioners of African Traditional Religion (ATR), Christians and Muslims. The major Christian celebrations of Christmas and Easter as well as Eid ul-Adha, which is the Festival of Sacrifice and Eid ul-Fitr, which is the End of Muslim Month of Fasting (Ramadan) celebrated by Muslims are recognized as national holidays. The respective ethnic groups also celebrate important traditional festivals. As already observed above, the religious composition of Ghana in the first post-independence population census of 1960 was made up of 41 percent Christians, 38 percent practitioners of ATR, 12 percent Muslims, and the rest (about 9 percent) had no religious affiliation. However, there have been dramatic changes over the years. According to the United States Department (2002), in the 2000 government census, it was found out that approximately 69 percent of the country's population was Christian, 16 percent Muslim, and 9 percent adhered to traditional indigenous religions. Other religions included the Baha'i Faith, Buddhism, Judaism, Hinduism, Shintoism, Ninchiren Shoshu Soka Gakkai, Sri Sathya Sai Baba Sera, Sat Sang, Eckanker, the Divine Light Mission, Hare Krishna, Rastafarianism, and other international faiths, as well as some separatist or spiritual churches which include elements of Christianity and traditional beliefs such as magic and divination. Zetahil, a practice unique to the country, combines elements of Christianity and Islam. There are no statistics available for the percentage of atheists in the country. Atheism does not have a strong presence since most persons have some spiritual and traditional beliefs. Christian denominations included Roman Catholic, Methodist, Anglican, Mennonite, Evangelical Presbyterian, Presbyterian, African Methodist Episcopal Zionist, Christian Methodist, Evangelical Lutheran, F'eden, numerous charismatic faiths, the Church of Jesus Christ of Latter-day Saints (Mormons), Seventh Day Adventist, Pentecostal, Baptist, and the Society of Friends.

The unifying organization of Christians in the country, of which the Catholic Church is not a member, is the *Ghana Christian Council*, founded in 1929. The Council serves as the link with the *World Council of Churches* and other ecumenical bodies. The *National Catholic Secretariat* established in 1960, also coordinates the different activities in the Archdioceses and Dioceses. These Christian organizations, concerned primarily with the spiritual affairs of their congregations, have occasionally acted in circumstances described by governments as political. Such was the case in 1991 when both the *Conference of Catholic Bishops* and the *Ghana Christian Council* called on the military Government of the *Provisional National Defense Council* (PNDC) to return the country to constitutional rule. Almost all major senior high schools in the country today, especially those that are exclusively boys' and girls' schools, are mission or church-related institutions. The Government requires that all students in public schools i.e. from primary up to junior high school level that are mission or Church-related attend a daily "assembly" or devotional service. However, in practice, this regulation is not enforced always. The service is Christian and includes the recital of The Lord's Prayer, Bible reading and sharing, and blessing. Students at the senior secondary school level are required to attend a similar assembly three times a week. Students attending government-administered boarding schools are required to attend a non-denominational service on Sundays (United States Department of State, 2002). With the above overview, there is no gainsaying the fact that the traditional society has undergone a dramatic change. The individual, as a member of this society, has not remained unaffected. In fact, one can say that he has many avenues to make life meaningful for himself.

The Individual in Ghana Today

The individual in traditional society seems to lack self-confidence and contentment. Unwittingly, an inferiority complex is his lot. This lack of self-confidence and contentment brings with it envy, irritability and lack of inner peace. The antidote for lack of contentment is the attainment of its opposite, namely self-confidence that grows out of courage and optimism. Filled with self-confidence, one has no need for complexes of contempt, rage or dissembling, and everywhere one moves one sees oneself as the equal of all the people about him, if not the superior, when one puts on airs. The Christian concept of the individual, as composed of body and soul, as a creature of God created by God in his own image and endowed with reason in virtue of which he has free will and must take the burden of moral responsibility for his own actions and charge to rule over creation, serves as the basis for what the individual needs to better understand himself in Ghana today. This is because not only are there elements in the Ghanaian understanding of the individual present in Christianity but also because the Christian principle about the individual will, when properly applied, go a long way to bridge cross-cultural differences in Ghana and beyond. Impressive to this is the exposition given by Leser (1984) of the important contribution of the Christian principles to the understanding and development of the individual despite its shortcomings.

The United States Catholic Conference (1998), writing on the Christian teaching on the individual in the light of the Catholic Church, asserts that *"Every human being is created in the image of God and is invaluable and worthy of respect as a member of the human family"* (The Principle of Human Dignity, *Reflections*, p.1). It sees the equality of all persons coming from their essential dignity." It also asserts that "human life at every stage of development and decline is precious and therefore worthy of protection and respect" (The Principle of Respect for Human Life, *Reflections*, pp.1-2). It points out to the fact that "the person is not only sacred but also social" (The Principle of Association, *Reflections*, p.4). Among his rights is the fact that he must "not be shut out from those institutions that are necessary for human fulfilment" (The Principle of Participation, *Reflections*, p.5). The individual is called to a "sense of moral responsibility for the protection of the environment" (The Principle of Stewardship, *Reflections*, p.6). We have the responsibility to care for the poor or the weak (The Principle of Preferential Protection for the Poor and Vulnerable, *Reflections*, p.5). Among other things, the idea that man is a substantive unity of spirit and material and that after death his spirit goes to a transcendental world known to the individual is already known, but what is lacking is the implication of this to the understanding of the individual and his relationship to other human beings. This aspect of spirit in the individual, which confirms his creation by a Supreme Being common to all cultures, as pointed out by Leser (1984), will serve as the basis of unity for the understanding of the individual not only among all the various tribes in Ghana but the world as a whole. This is because the Christian teaching on the individual locates him in the "family of human beings". This spirit differentiates the human being from other creatures of the creator and not the human being from other human beings. It is the entity that Scheler refers to in German as "*der Geist*" meaning the spirit. The individual by virtue of this spirit has dignity and is equal to others and must respect them as such and expect respect from them. By virtue of this spirit, he has freedom to do his will. To be free here means to do what is good because the spirit in the individual makes him naturally good and capable of knowing what is good. This explains why the individual does all he can alone or in a group to achieve the best for himself. By virtue of this spirit he can think, and in cooperation with other individuals with his kind of spirit, he finds fulfilment in life. Like other individuals, he has basic rights which include the right to life. The implication of this is that we have no right to violate others' natural rights to life, liberty, and possessions. No one has the right to use others for his selfish end. We have no right to destroy ourselves and we have no right to harm others. On the other hand, we have the responsibility to preserve the rest of mankind (Onyeocha, 1997, n. p.).

The spirit in the individual, which is called the soul, makes the individual the only creature who can, after a life in this world, hope to participate in an eternal life that is far more important than the temporal life that he lives here. As has already been discussed above, the Ghanaian tradition believes in life after death in the world of ancestors. The defect of this idea in the traditional set up is the fact that the individual is believed to continue his work on earth in the world of the dead. For example, a servant in this life remains a servant in the next; a king in this life remains a king in the world of the ancestors. Such a belief gladdens the heart of the privileged and saddens that of the unprivileged. But the Christian principle promises a life of eternal glory of beatific vision for those who live lives expected of them. This principle, among others, gives hope to an individual, who because of certain physical disabilities does not find fulfilment in this life. When he accepts himself as an individual with all his traits, he can, in communion with other individuals, work for a happy life, as they show respect for one another. When this happens, we can understand him as that political animal, who according to Aristotle, must belong to a state with laws in order to live a meaningful and happy life (Graham, n. d.). It is important that the individual understands his membership in a state as a citizen. This is because unlike the development of a state presented by Aristotle as a natural development from the family to the village and then to the state and by Hegel as development from the family to the civil community and then to the state, that of Ghana can be said to have moved from tribal communities to the state. The problem with this is that the civil aspect of life was not well developed before the state was formed. But it must be made clear that the tribes themselves agreed to form a nation. As a nation with a constitution, an individual must be a recognised constituent of the state, not a tribe. Therefore, he should be seen as a citizen in a democratic state which sees all citizens as equal in theory.

The individual must be made to understand the difference between loyalty to the state of which he is a member and membership to the tribe. This will, among other things, play down tribal tendencies which seem to stress the importance of a people vis-à-vis other people. This will also encourage the individual to value himself directly as a person having the same political right like all other individuals, who, like him, are all human beings that have come together for the sake of living well. He is an individual, who through the exercise of his political right, has given consent of some kind to the state so that he can fully live his life in the society in which he finds himself. As such, he shall be sacrificed for the end of the other. As a political animal in a democratic state, who can rule and be ruled, as Rousseau put it, he must guard against being dominated by others or seeking to dominate others. When he is aware that it is not the tribes but individuals like him who form the state, he will choose a person who will rule him not because he belongs to his tribe or is related to him by blood. What must be clear to us following our discussions so far is that the Western system of thought regarding the individual and his well-being, which majority of Ghanaians apply to their lives as against the traditional system of thought, has come to stay. We must make use of what is good for the individual. In line with the constitution, Government must take into consideration individual welfare through which societal welfare can be ensured. The constitution, according to Aristotle and Hegel, must rule. As such, the rights and responsibilities of the individual must be defined by the constitution to avoid the stress on individual responsibilities to the neglect of rights as found in the tribal set up under the pretext of stressing the common good. On the economic front, without neglecting the idea of working in community, the individual should be made aware of his right to survive. In line with this he must be made aware of the fact that he has talents that he can make use of to ensure his survival. As explained above, we are all traders and we enter into contract to ensure our survival.

Consequently, contracts freely reached must be respected or observed. One should give out something and take something in return. This will check the traditional system of working in communities where people work for relatives without a just pay. The Government must ensure that agreements voluntarily reached are enforced. In addition to this, with a third of Ghanaians professing the Christian faith, I think that aspects of Weber's (1992) work, which propagates the idea that traditional disdain for acquisitive effort shall be diminished, while hard work and frugality shall be given a stronger religious or moral sanction, will help the individual from his economic plight. In this case, the idea that all men must work, even the rich, because to work is the will of God, must be encouraged as moral. Furthermore, the conception that each individual had a "calling" from God to a certain job will facilitate the division of labour while implying a moral imperative to work. Work in a chosen occupation will be encouraged with an attitude of service to God and community. Work viewed as a calling will avoid placing greater dignity on one job than another, it will approve of working diligently to achieve maximum profits, require reinvestment of profits back into one's business. Everybody does what he can do best for his survival .This will lead to contentment that will in effect prevent the flow into the city centres that are not able to cater for the economic needs and social behaviour of the individual. In line with this, the decolonisation of certain aspect of the colonial mentality put forward by Wiredu (1992, p.67) will be of help. The idea that the best comes from the Western countries by the media as capable of solving all problems must be discouraged. The individual should be made to understand that like other individuals he can find life meaningful wherever he is. With the understanding that he can achieve what others elsewhere have achieved, the Government should encourage decentralization and investment where ever the situation allows so that modern facilities would not only be cited in the cities, thereby luring people into the cities but could be enjoyed everywhere. To achieve all this, education is seen as important in the schools, at home and in the churches to mention but a few. As pointed out above, in the field of education much is being done in Ghana. In recent times, as pointed out above Government is aimed at providing basic education for all; there is education and training for skill development with emphasis on science, technology and creativity; and there is higher education for the development of middle and top-level manpower requirements. With the availability of these facilities, the individual must be educated in his conception of himself and of other individuals. He needs to know what he needs all this for, namely the service of mankind for his own good and the good of other individuals. Knowledge of this will ensure respect for the other and ensure mutual trust and cross-cultural cooperation and avoidance of nepotism in politics, in business and job distribution. Like Aristotle's suggestion on education that democrats must study oligarchs, education in Ghana must be geared towards knowledge about both foreign and indigenous values. This will help the individual evaluate both indigenous and alien values. In the light of the crisis in our identity, one important role of education is to serve as an agent of social reconstruction through the carefully selected values that it transmits. This, among others, will help the citizens have a clear notion of the type and nature of indigenous and alien values that impinge upon their experience as individuals and as groups. Accordingly, this will help the individual (1) to work out principles for selecting from our various cultural traditions, values that he will need in order to cope effectively with the demands of progress and modernization. Some of the needed values are: hard work, co-operation, discipline, self-correction, initiative, respect for evidence and verifiable knowledge and the experimental method of solving problems; (2) to develop and raise the individual's consciousness of the presence of the creative dynamic life power in him, in others and in society, and to help him make disciplined use of this energy, (3) to help the (individual) child appreciate the value of change and growth in life and to grow through learning. This is the surest way to free the child from the hold of any unworthy traditionalism or authority; (4) to help the individual use values as the basis of all his choices and actions and to equip him with the ability to develop new values in new problem situations; (5) to help the individual affirm his indigenous cultural roots so that he/she does not become alienated.

The necessity of the above is due to the fact that even though the Ghanaian culture has responded to great changes in its physical and social environments by creative adaptations and adjustments over the years, today the changes and challenges facing the individual in this culture are most acute and most pervasive. The perplexities caused have, to some extent, served as the occasion for devising programmatic social theories and cultural proposals, in whose light certain features of the culture, which are held to be non-traditional, are to be curbed because they are thought of as corrupting the individual. These are deplored because they are still thought of as being unauthentic and alien. For others, however, these same features are, with some caution and conscious purpose, to be integrated and internalized, and welcomed as triggers of beneficent evolution and catalysts of progress. If the internal similarities are sufficiently acted upon by elements of cultures from Europe, Asia, and the Americas, which are present in Africa and belong to the historical experience of African cultures, the similarities can be enhanced and can eventually goad the irreversible flowering of the individual. There is no doubt that elements of cultures from Asia, Europe, and the Americas are already well known to the majority of Ghanaians. There are millions among whom these are admired and they are learning or are ready to learn from these elements.

The scientific, technological, literary, and artistic content of these cultures, the goods which they have generated, and the high degree of self-expression which this content permits, all find great favour with the individual. These find expression today in his political concepts and organization, in economic practice and structure, in educational institutions, methods, and curricula, in employment patterns and labour practices, in agricultural crops, farming methods, and husbandry, in the forms and uses of leisure, in music, dance, literature, and the arts, in family relations and practices, in the rites of birth, marriage, and death, in language, belief, values, dress, and manners.

Educating the individual on them rather than throwing them aboard will help the individual work out principles for selecting the values he will need in order to cope effectively with the demands of modern living, while maintaining at the same time the integrity for his indigenous cultural identity Like many others that see the dynamics of consciousness, the will to progress, the skills and the psychological attitudes necessary for progress as necessary. Dzobo (1992, p.226) is convinced and thinks it can only accrue from widespread education based on soundly designed curricula. Universal, compulsory, and consequently, free education for all pupils and students in urban as well as rural areas will be the means to bring all into the context of the human family across regional and national lines.

Conclusion

From the above we have seen that the individual Ghanaian adopts the Western concepts, as he carries within himself a base of traditional culture upon which profoundly wrenching demands are made. We see an individual who is not able to identify himself clearly. We see him confronted with an important decision to make, namely whether to accept modern civilization at his own expense, or to do so on his own terms, or to reject everything completely and slip back into the limbo of the past. We see reaction to save him pouring out from all angles. There are those who think he should return to his roots, there are those who think he should adopt the Western style of life, and there are those who think he seems to call for a kind of compromise. With majority of Ghanaians educated in Western concept and with a third professing the Christian faith this chapter advocates that the individual in Ghana today understands himself as a person made up of body and soul who is created by God in his own image and endowed with reason, and that by virtue of this he has free will and must take the burden of moral responsibility for his own actions and rule over creation. This is because not only are there elements in the Ghanaian understanding of the individual present in Christianity but also because Christian principles about the individual, when properly applied, will go a long way to give meaning not found anywhere for now to the individual in this country. This meaning is expressed in his relationship to others as their equal who must be respected. He has life after death which promises him a better life than he is experiencing now. In politics, he, like other individuals, contributes to the formation of the state and in the economic field, he is a trader who has talent for his survival, among others. We realise that for the individual to understand this he needs education.

GENERAL CONCLUSION

The subject of this work has been to look at how the Western social philosophical concept of individualism and society has influenced and continues to influence the individual in Ghana, and how giving worth to the individual in Ghana can lead to self-appreciation and contentment. The work tries to demonstrate that the encounter with the Western world brought about a dramatic change in the individual as far as his membership of the traditional society is concerned. His base of traditional culture, which engulfs beliefs about the nature of human beings as members of his society, about the ethics which should regulate human behaviour within the family and its extensions, as well as beliefs, which regulate general behaviour towards members of the same society, and even higher beliefs which inspire his ethics are irreversibly impregnated at various levels by elements of foreign concepts, some of which were imposed on him when he was colonized, while others were sought and acquired. As a result, the individual thinks, learns, works, conceives his hopes and aspirations within a new belief system which comes with its own axioms and postulates as well as its own norms and its own ethics.

This has, in no small way, affected his relationship to other individuals, his responsibilities to the group and his attitude to nature. The individual is now in a kind of crisis, which is traced to and identified by the fact that the dominance of this colonialism was incomplete. In other words, the indigenous modes of thought and action were not totally eclipsed by colonialism. This has ensured that even the educated individual has never been completely cut off from his culture. The said crisis haunts him on the social, political, ideological and psychological front to mention but a few. It haunts him in the clothes he wears, the food he eats, the language he speaks, the way he worships, the way he rules or is ruled, acts or reacts.

The individual in Ghana today continues to carry within himself a traditional culture upon which profoundly wrenching demands are made. We see him confronted with a decision whether to accept modern civilization at his own expense, or to do so on his own terms, or to reject everything completely and slip back into the limbo of the past. Whiles governments look for solution in the West, some individuals and groups look for solutions in West and in traditional cultures. In order to avert the crisis, some scholars call for total decolonization through which people's colonial mentality becomes a thing of the past, while others call for a return to the roots. These people are convinced of the fact that what is required for authentic identity, self-discovery, self-appreciation and contentment is that one's decision or choice should be based on one's own conscious reflection. It calls for an effort by the individual to reconstruct in his or her own mind an order of reasoning that reflects and interprets a pattern of order in nature - an effort that leads to a search for authority in natural law which, advocates the fact that man has a natural inclination and ability to know the truth and so can research to appreciate himself. For the individual in Ghana to reach this end the author sees the contribution of Western philosophy as a useful and helpful supplement leading to the individual's self-affirmation. In line with this, the first chapter of the work dealt with the empowerment of the individual over the centuries by Western philosophy beginning with the Greeks. Here we see the individual making progress by finding solutions to problems posed by his environment, as he takes recourse to some gods or mythology and makes use of reason. With Christianity his relationship to the supernatural world is made clear. He is a creature of God, created in His image. In Chapter two, we observed that the Western philosophical empowerment of the individual, which set out to make the individual more important than any other living thing led to individualism in the Western world. It is that political and social philosophy that places high value on the freedom of the individual and generally stresses the self-directed, self-contained, and comparatively unrestrained individual or ego. In line with the above we considered the place of individual in the western society with particular reference to the social contract theory in the eyes of Thomas Hobbes, John Locke, and Jean-Jacques Rousseau. The conclusion we arrive at is that the individual like other individuals form the state. They have given their consent to the state and so the state must protect their interest so that they can live well. To do justice to the topic the third chapter looked at the Ghanaian traditional concept of the individual. It is clear that the systematic discussion of the development of the individual in the west is lacking in the Ghanaian context because of lack of literature. The Akan concept of man is, therefore, looked at and supposed to represent the concept of the individual in Ghana bearing in mind that differences of details may exist from one tribe to the other. In general terms, therefore, the individual was looked at in line with the social, economic, and political organization of the traditional society, among others.

In the process, we realised a stress on the ontological primacy of the community, the natural sociality of the individual, the organic character of the relations between individuals, and the overarching importance of the community as the prerequisite for the total well-being or complete realization of the nature of the individual. He owes his existence to other people, including those of past generations and his contemporaries. He is simply part of the whole. The community is what therefore makes, creates or produces the individual. Physical birth is not seen as enough to make an individual what he will become. The relationship between him and the society is mutual and interdependent. That is to say each has a mutual responsibility for the other. He is seen as an inherently communal being, embedded in a context of social relationships and interdependence, never as an isolated, atomic individual. Social relationships become necessary and not conditional. The individual does not voluntarily choose to enter into human community.

This implies that community life is not optional for any individual, and he must, therefore, not live in isolation from other persons. By now we have tried to distinguish between two main philosophical conceptions of the individual and society. Both of them attempt to interpret the fact that the human being is understood as an individual having spiritual life, containing in himself an awareness of self-identity and capable of acting. He realizes himself as a social agent engaged in various areas of social life in relation to other persons in society. For obvious reasons, we cannot conclude that the West is solely individualistic. It also represents thought that emphasizes that the individual is a primary human reality and affirms that one's social relations have an external or peripheral character rather than an essential character. As an individual each person is what he is in his own right; he is a unique individual. On the other hand, the traditional Ghanaian society will represent the contrary thought that sees the essence of the individual consisting in mutuality, interpersonal relations or involvement in the life of the community or society. Although no society can be characterized entirely by one or the other system, the faith of the traditional West in free enterprise, the virtues of self-reliance and self-improvement all rest on a sense of competitive individualism. We need only to look at awards such as the Academy Awards popularly called the Oscars that are awards for artistic and technical merit in the film industry or Best Teacher of the Year Awards and we will be reminded of the countless ways this society singles out the special worth of individual achievement. As we have already seen, whiles the West fosters independence and individual achievement, the traditional society fosters interdependence and group success. Unlike the West that promotes self-expression, individual thinking and personal choice, the traditional system promotes adherence to norms, respect for authority and elders and group consensus. Whereas the West is associated with egalitarian relationships and flexibility in roles, the traditional community is associated with stable, hierarchical roles dependent on gender, family background, and age. Whereas the West is associated with private property and individual ownership, the tribal community is associated with shared property and group ownership. In the traditional society, children are expected to understand and act on a strong sense of responsibility toward the group, the family, and the community. They are also taught to respect their elders as the sources of knowledge and wisdom for their community. In this community, self-worth and esteem are not defined chiefly in terms of individual achievement. They are rather derived from "the performance of self-sacrificing acts that create social links and bonds". In sharp contrast, young people in individualistic societies are typically expected to make educational and occupational choices that develop their own potential not necessarily with any consideration for how their success would benefit their families. We also saw that the West and the traditional societies reflect fundamentally different perceptions about knowledge, cognition, and social development. Individualistic societies do not see knowledge and wisdom as the special province of designated elders. The self-expression children commonly exhibit toward adults would be interpreted as a lack of proper respect in a traditional society. The matter is not that one or another philosophical theory is better or worse with respect to its consistency and to the extent to which it corresponds to the facts of human reality. Human experience is far too complex to fit neatly into any conceptual scheme. No society is all one thing or another. Each "strikes a particular balance between individual and society, between independence and interdependence. Even within a particular ethnic group, members are extremely diverse. Our concern is what happens to the individual in Ghana, when he encounters the West. The fourth chapter shows that the individual is affected in a dramatic way.

In the encounter, the traditional societies were penetrated by a new brand of thought system introduced by their colonial masters. We observe that these thought systems alter the force and direction of the host cultures. They alter the social relations and the rationale underlying the organization of traditional societies. They also introduced new ways of doing things and new reasons for doing them. In short, the encounter changed in many different ways at one and the same time relations between individuals and relations with the environment. This intermingling of cultures, through influences of politics, economics, religion, literature, art, and education, to mention but a few, resulted in identity crisis of the individual. The individual finds himself torn between two worlds. Thinking, learning, working and conceiving his hopes and aspirations within a new belief system, which comes with its own axioms and postulates, its own norms, and its own ethics has in no small way affected his relationship to other individuals, his responsibilities to the group and his attitude to nature. Since most influential philosophical theories of man appear more compatible and complementary than contradictory, there are more areas in which they agree than contradict. It must be made clear that the search for the place of the individual in society is a search for a means and not an end. To find the place of the individual in society is to find a means to progress toward union with others. In line with the above, the last chapter, after considering efforts by some scholars to solve the problem, tries to look at the individual in light of both concepts with the simple reason that culture is dynamic. We can take whatever is useful and applicable in any culture for our development. Furthermore, it is not for nothing that our forefathers accepted the Western culture. As pointed out above, some tribes voluntarily accepted British protection so that they can live in peace and be protected from aggressive neighbours. In effect, certain customs like ritual murder sanctioned by the gods of the tribes, which deprived the individual of his right to exist, were abolished. Having tried to understand the individual in the light of Christian principles backed by the Ghanaian concept of the individual with particular reference to the spiritual component, which differentiates him from other living things but identifies him with other individuals, a concept that will ensure self-appreciation and respect for the other, the work calls for the education of the individual in both Western and traditional values with the hope that the individual can make the best use of what is best in both cultures. We continue to see this self-realisation made extremely difficult because of the colonial mentality that people have, and for that matter many individuals in Ghana today remain convinced that making it to the West will solve all problems. It is hoped that with the help of education the individual will come to appreciate himself more and more and make life pleasant for himself wherever he finds himself. Although many problems remain unresolved and many questions remain unanswered, I hope this work provides a starting point for a comprehensive social philosophical understanding by the individual as he struggles to discover himself in the Ghanaian society.

REFERENCES

ENCYCLOPAEDIAE AND DICTIONARIES

American Peoples Encyclopedia (1968). A Modern Reference Work Grolier Incorporated.

Audi, R. (1999). *The Cambridge Dictionary of Philosophy (2nd Ed.).* Cambridge University Press.

The Catholic Encyclopedia (2003). https://www.newadvent. org/cathen/i.htm

Encarta World English Dictionary (1999). London: Bloomsbury Publishing Plc.

Encyclopedia Britannica CD Deluxe Edition 1994-2001.

BOOKS

Abraham, W. E. (1992). "Crisis in African Cultures". In *Person and Community: Ghanaian*

Philosophical Studies, I. (Contemporary Change, Series II.) Kwasi Wiredu and Kwame

Gyekye (Eds.). Washington, D.C. The Council for Research in Values and Philosophy.

Adler, A. (1956). *The Individual Psychology of Alfred Adler: A Systematic Presentation*

In Selection from His Writings. H. L. Ansbacher & R. R. Ansbacher (Eds.). New York: Basic Books.

Aristotle (n. d.). *The Politics.* Trans. by T.A. Sinclair. (1962). Revised by Trevor J Saunders. (1981). Great Britain: Penguin Books. pp. 59-60.

Assimeng, M. (1999). *Social Structure of Ghana. A Study in Persistence and Change.*

Tema: Ghana Publishing Corporation.

Author Unknown. (1997). *Tradition and Modernity Philosophical, Reflections on the*

African Experience. London: Oxford University Press.

Author Unknown. (1987). *An Essay on African Philosophical Thought.* London: Cambridge University Press.

Author Unknown. (1980). *Philosophy and an African Culture.* Cambridge University Press.

Bader, E. (1991). *Christliche Sozialreform*. Beitraege zur Sozialphilosophie in einer veraenderten Welt. Freiburg, Basel & Wien: Herder Verlag.

Curtin, P. D. (1972). *The Atlantic Slave Trade: A Census.* Wisconsin University Press.

Dzobo, N. K. (1992). *"The Image of Man in Africa"*. In Person and Community: Ghanaian Philosophical Studies, I. (Contemporary Change, Series II.) Kwasi Wiredu and Kwame Gyekye, eds. Washington, D.C. The Council for Research in Values and Philosophy.

Dzobo, N. K. (1992). "Values in a Changing Society: Man, Ancestors and God". In *Person and Community: Ghanaian Philosophical Studies, I. (Contemporary Change, Series II.)* Kwasi Wiredu and Kwame Gyekye, eds. Washington, D.C. The Council for Research in Values and Philosophy.

Grayling, A. C. (1998). Philosophy 2 Further Through the Subject. London: Oxford University Press.

Gyekye, K. (2010). Annals of Humanities and Development Studies. Vol. 1. No. 2 on *Problems of Self-Definition and Development in Africa: A Critique.*

Hampton, J. (1986). Hobbes and the Social Contract Tradition. Cambridge University Press.

Hegel, G W F. (1996). Philosophy of Rights. (Trans. by S W Dyde). *Great Books in Philosophy*. New York: Prometheus Books. pp. 164-350.

Hoogvelt, A. (n. d.). *Globalization and the Post-Colonial world. The New Political Economy of Development*. Baltimore, Maryland: The John Hopkins University Press.

Jansz, J. (1991). *Person Self and Moral Demands, Individualism Contested by Collectivism*. Holland: Door.

Khudadjie, J. N. (1995). *Moral Renewal in Ghana: Ideals, Realities and Possibilities*. Asempa Publishers: Accra

Leser, N. (1984). *Sozialphilosophie*. Wien: Böhlau Verlag.

Macfarlane, A. (1978). *The Origins of English Individualism: The Family, Property and*

Social Transition. Blackwell, Oxford.

Macpherson, C. B. (1962). *The Political Theory of Possessive Individualism: Hobbes to*

Locke. New York: Oxford University Press.

Mbiti, J. S. (1969). *African Religion and Philosophy*. London: Heineman Educational Books.

Mbiti, J. S. (1991). *Introduction to African Religion*. African Writers Series. Heinemann.

Montaigne, M. (1580). *Essais*. Simon Millanges: Jean Richer.

Nkrumah, K. (1964). *Consciencism: Philosophy and ideology for decolonization and development with particular reference to the African revolution*. London: Heinemann.

Oquaye, M. (1980). *Politics in Ghana1972-1979*. Ghana: Tornado Publications.

Quarcoopome, T. N. O. (1987). *West African Traditional Religion*. Ibadan: African Universities Press.

Rousseau, J.-J. (1755). *Discourse on the Origin and Foundation of Inequality among Mankind*. Published by Marc-Michel Rey: Holland.

Rousseau, J.-J (1762). *The Social Contract*. Tozer, H. J., (trans.) (1998). Great Britain: Wordsworth Edition Limited.

Russell, B. (1979). *A History of Western Philosophy*. Counterpoint ed. London: George

Allen &Unwin Publisher.

Sarpong, P. K. (1998). *Dear Nana. Letters to My Ancestors*. Takoradi, Ghana: Franciscan Publications.

Sarpong, P. K. (1974). *Ghana in Retrospect. Some Aspects of Ghanaian Culture.* Tema: Ghana Publishing Corporation.

Scheler, M. (1928). *Die Stellung des Menschen im Kosmos.* Felix Meiner Verlag: Hamburg

Scheler, M. (1913). *Der Formalismus in der Ethik und die Materiale Wertethik.* Felix Meiner Verlag: Hamburg.

Stirner, M. (1993). *The Ego and Its Own: The Case of the Individual Against Authority* London: Rebel Press.

Triandis, H. C. (1995). *Individualism and Collectivism.* Boulder, Colo.: Westview Press.

United States Catholic Conference (1998). *Sharing Catholic Social Teaching: Challenges and Directions: reflections of the U.S. Catholic Bishops.* Issue 5, Part 281.

Values in Changing Societies. (1992). Man, Ancestors and God in George F. Mclean Person and Community Ghanaian Philosophical Studies I. Washington D.C.

Weber, M. (1992). *The Protestant Ethic and the Spirit of Capitalism.* Translated by Talcott Parsons with an introduction by Anthony Giddens. Routledge: London and New York

Webster, J. B., Boahen, A. A. & Tidy, M. (1980). *The Revolutionary Years: West Africa since 1800 (Growth of African Civilisation).* Longman Group Ltd.

ONLINE BOOKS AND ARTICLES

Asante, M. K. (1980). *Afrocentricity: The Theory of Social Change*. Retrieved from http://www.asante. net/articles/guadalupe-asante.html [accessed on 26th April, 2004]

Britain and the Gold Coast: The Early Years. Retrieved from http://www.country-studies.com/ghana/ britain-and-the-gold-coast:-the-early-years.html [accessed on 3rd April, 2004]

Economic Indicators. Retrieved from http://ghanaweb.com/ GhanaHomePage/economy/statistics.php [accessed on 12th June, 2003]

Ghana: a Country Study/Federal Research Division, Library of Congress (1995). *Report on Ghana Data* as of November 1994. Retrieved http://www.ghana. co.uk/history/and_and_people.htm [accessed on 17th July, 2002]

Ghana, Christianity Land and People. Retrieved from http://www.ghana.co.uk/religion/religions_group/ christian.htm. [accessed on 12th June, 2003]

Ghana Colonial Administration data 1994-2004 in Country Studies. The Library of Congress.

Ghana Country Study And Guide: Society, The Library of Congress- Country Studies in reference.allrefer.com/

country-guide-study/Ghana/ghana7 [accessed on 22nd April, 2004]

Ghana, Economic And Social Development data 1994-2004.

Globalization: Threat or Opportunity? By IMF Staff April 12, 2000 (Corrected January 2002). Retrieved from http://www.imf.org/external/np/exr/ib/2000/041200. htm [accessed on 12th June, 2003]

Graham, A. R. *The Traditional Self In A Changing Society.* Centre For Education and National Development, The George Washington University, D.C. Retrieved from http://lautbry.tripod.com/cpce/index.htm [accessed on 3rd April, 2004]

Health. Retrieved from http://www.ourghana.com/ aboutghana/fact-file.php [accessed on 22nd April, 2004]

History, Early European Contact and the Slave Trade. Retrieved from http://www.ghanaweb.com/ GhanaHomePage/history/slave-trade.php [accessed on 21st July, 2002]

Hobbes, T. (n. d.). *Leviathan.* Retrieved from http:// www.4literature.net/Thomas_Hobbes/Leviathan [accessed on 17th July, 2002]

Individualisms, *Catholic Encyclopaedia.*Retrieved from http://www.newadvent.org/cathen/07761a.htm [accessed on 3rd April, 2004]

Kuzmickas, B. *The Person, Society and The State* Chapter Vii. Retrieved from http://www.crvp.org/book/Series01/I-6/chapter_vii [accessed on 17th July, 2002]

Mackenzie, J. *Deadly Voyage.* Retrieved from http://www.amazon.com/exec/obidos/tg/detail/ [accessed on 3rd April, 2004]

Mbiti, J. S. (1981). *African Tradition and the Christian God.* Retrieved from https://doi.org/10.1177/239693938100500121 [accessed on 22nd April, 2004]

Oduyoye, M. A. *The African Experience of God through the eyes of an Akan Woman.* Retrieved from www.theology.i.e/theologians/ecumenis.htm [accessed in 21st July, 2002]

Onyeocha, I. M. (1997). *Africa: The Question of Identity: A Philosophical Reflection on Africa.* Retrieved from http://www.crvp.org/book/Series02/II-3/chapter_iii.htm. [accessed on 17th July, 2002]

Pink, A. W. (n. d.) *The Doctrine of Justification.* Retrieved from http://www.gregwolf.com/pink/justification/justification.htm [accessed on 12th June, 2003]

Plato. *Republic Book VII.* Retrieved from http://www.gradesaver.com/ClassicNotes/Titles/republic/about.html. [accessed on 17th July, 2002]

Ross, K. L. *History of Philosophy. The Origin of Philosophy: The Attributes of Mythic/Mythopoeic Thought.* Retrieved from http://www.friesian.com/greek.htm [accessed on 17th July, 2002]

Religion Christianity and Islam. Retrieved from http://atheism.about.com/library/world/AJ/bl_GhanaChristianityIslam.htm [Accessed on 21st July, 2002]

Report by Ministry of Education. Retrieved from http://www.ghana.edu.gh/people/whatsNew.html [accessed on 22nd April, 2004]

Stata, R. (1992). *What is Individualism?* Retrieved from http://www.vix.com/objectivism/Writing/RaymieStata/WhatIsIndividualism.html [accessed on 22nd April, 2004]

Steiner, R. (1989). *Individualism in Philosophy (Der Individualismus in der Philosophie).* Retrieved from http://wn.rsarchive.org/Articles/IndPhi_essay.html [accessed on 22nd April, 2004]

Stein, H. T. *Some basic principles of individual psychology* (by Sophia J De Vries) (Originally published in the "Individual Psychology Bulletin," Vol. 9, 1951.) Retrieved from http://ourworld.compuserve.com/homepages/hstein/basic.htm [accessed on 22nd April, 2004]

The European Union Constitution. Retrieved from http://www.unizar.es/euroconstitucion/Home.htm [accessed on 21st July, 2002]

The Guardian, 06 Dec 2002. Retrieved from http://www.guardian.co.uk/airlines/story/0,1371,854754,00.html [accessed on 12th June, 2003]

Tocqueville, A. de. (1840). Democracy in America. Volume II section II. The Americans combat individualism by the principle of self-interest rightly understood. Retrieved from http://xroads.virginia.edu/~HYPER/DETOC/ch2_08.htm. [accessed on 21st July, 2002]

Tyehimba, R. (2004). Demonizing in the name of Christianity. Retrieved from http://www.cultural-expressions.com/thesis/demonizing.htm [accessed on April 3, 2004]

United States Department of State (2002). *International Religious Freedom Report* – Ghana 2002. Retrieved from http://www.state.gov/g/drl/rls/irf/2004/35360.htm [accessed on 3rd April, 2004]

Waterman, A. S. (1981). Individualism and interdependence. *American Psychologist*, 36(7), 762-773. Retrieved from https://doi.org/10.1037/0003-066X.36.7.762 [accessed on 22nd April, 2004]

Wiley, D. (1981). *Using "Tribe" and "Tribalism" Categories to Misunderstand Africa, African Studies Centre.* Michigan State University. Retrieved from http://

africa.wisc.edu/outreach/units/tribe.html [accessed on 3rd April, 2004]

Wiredu, K. (1998). *Toward Decolonizing African Philosophy and Religion. The Online Journal for African Studies.* Retrieved from http://www.clas.ufl.edu/africa/asq/v1/4/3.htm [accessed on 3rd April, 2004]

World Factbook: *Ghana-People*. Retrieved from http://www.cia.gov/cia/publications/factbook/geos/gh.html#Econ [accessed on 21st July, 2002]

GLOSSARY

Acculturation, a change in the cultural behaviour and thinking of an individual or group through contact with another culture.

Adlerian psychology, Adlerian psychology and psychotherapy are both humanistic and goal oriented. They emphasize the individual's strivings for success, connectedness with others, and contributions to society as being hallmarks of mental health.

Aristocracy, people of noble families or the highest social class. A government of a country by a small group of people, especially a hereditary nobility.

Aristotelian, expressing or based on the ideas of the Greek philosopher Aristotle. A follower of Aristotle's philosophy.

Capitalism, an economic system based on the private ownership of the means of production and distribution of goods, characterized by a free competitive market and motivation by profit.

235

Chauvinism, an excessive or prejudiced loyalty to a particular gender, group, or cause

Classical Greek philosophy, a philosophy that arose and flourished in the 6th century BC and continued throughout the Hellenistic period and the period in which Greece and most Greek-inhabited lands were part of the Roman empire.

Collectivism, a system of control and ownership of factories and farms and of the means of production and distribution of products by a nation's people.

Consciencism, Nkrumaism (sometimes *Consciencism*) is an African socialist political ideology based on the thinking and writing of Kwame Nkrumah. In his concept of *Consciencism,* Dr Kwame Nkrumah draws together strands from the three main traditions that make up the African conscience: the Euro-Christian, the Islamic and the original African.

Das Erkennen, recognition

Decentralization, to reorganize something such as a political unit so that power is shifted from a central or upper location to another, less central place.

Der Geist, the Spirit

Dialectical, the tension that exists between two conflicting or interacting forces, elements or ideas. [Hegelian process] the process, in Hegelian and Marxist thought, in which two apparently opposed ideas, the thesis and antithesis, become combined in a unified whole, the synthesis.

Dogmatism, the tendency to express strongly held opinions in a way that suggests they should be accepted without question.

Dualism, a philosophical theory based on the idea of opposing concepts, especially the theory that human beings are made up of two independent constituents, the body and the mind, soul.

Enlightenment, an 18th century intellectual movement in western Europe that emphasized reason and science in philosophy and in the study of human culture and the natural world.

Evangelicalism, a Protestant movement of the Christian church whose members believe in the authority of the Bible and salvation through the personal acceptance of Jesus Christ.

Fetishism, excessive or obsessive attachment or devotion to something.

Feudalism, [medieval social system] the legal and social system that existed in medieval Europe, in which vassals held land from lords in exchange for military service.

Freiheit, freedom

Gemeinschaft, community

Gesellschaft, Society

Globalization, the process by which social institutions become adopted on a global scale. The process by which a business or company becomes international or starts operating at an international level.

Humanism, the secular cultural and intellectual movement of the Renaissance that spread throughout Europe as a result of the rediscovery of the arts and philosophy of the ancient Greeks and Romans.

Inculturation, the gradual acquisition of the characteristics and norms of a culture or group by a person, another culture, etc.

Intersubjectivity, the psychological relation between people.

Ionian, a member of an ancient Greek people who lived in Attica around the 10th century BC, before spreading out to many of the coastal regions and islands of the Aegean. They established important cultural and trading centres in their new settlements.

Mawu, the Ewe word for the Supreme Being (God).

Meditation, (Meditations on First Philosophy, in which the existence of God and the immortality of the soul are demonstrated). A philosophical treatise by René Descartes first published in Latin in 1641. The book is made up of 6 (six) meditations.

Mechanistic atomism, a miraculous conception of the world, to atoms which just miraculously behave in a certain way.

Metaphor of the Cave, also called *The Allegory of the Cave,* is a metaphor designed to illustrate human perception, ideologies, illusions, opinions, ignorance and sensory appearances.

Miscegenation, sexual relations between people of different races, especially of different skin colours, leading to the birth of children. The word as means a marriage or cohabitation between people of different races.

Monad, in the metaphysics of Leibniz, an indivisible indestructible unit that is the basic element of reality and microcosm of it.

Monolithic, massive, uniform in character, and slow to change.

Neo-platonism, a philosophical system combining Platonism with mysticism and Judaic and Christian ideas and positing one source for all existence, developed by Plotinus and his followers in the 3rd century AD.

Onyame, an Akan word for a smaller or lesser god

Onyankopon, an Akan word for the Supreme Being (in Christianity called God)

Pan-African, relating to the nations of Africa, collectively or in cooperation with one another, or advocating freedom and independence for African people.

Panyarring, it was the practice of seizing and holding persons until the repayment of debt or resolution of a dispute which became a common activity along the Atlantic coast of Africa in the 18th and 19th centuries.

Parochialism, concerned only with narrow local concerns without any regard for more general or wider ideas.

Platonic, relating to Plato or his philosophy. The philosophy is the theory that both physical objects and instances of qualities are recognizable because of their common relationship to an abstract form or idea.

Prisoner's Dilemma, is a standard example of a game analysed in game theory that shows why two completely rational individuals might not cooperate, even if it appears that it is in their best interests to do so.

Reformation, the 16th century religious movement in Europe that set out to reform some of the doctrines and practices of the Roman Catholic Church and resulted in the development of Protestantism.

Relativism, the belief that concepts such as right and wrong, goodness and badness, or truth and falsehood are not absolute but change from culture to culture and situation to situation.

Renaissance, the period in European history from about the 14th to 16th centuries regarded as marking the end of the Middle Ages and featuring major cultural and artistic change. The new emphasis on individualism and secularism at this time led to the Reformation.

Republic, a Socratic dialogue, authored by Plato around 375 BC, concerning justice, the order and character of the just city-state, and the just man.

Scholasticism, a medieval theological and philosophical system of learning based on the authority of St. Augustine and other leaders of the early Christian Church, and on the works of Aristotle. It sought to bridge the gap between religion and reason.

Sophistry, a method of argumentation that seems clever but is actually flawed or dishonest.

Theophoric names, they are names containing the name of God or god in whose care the individual is entrusted.

Totem, an object, animal, plant, or other natural phenomenon revered as a symbol of a tribe and often used in rituals among some tribal or other traditional groups of people.

Utilitarianism, the ethical doctrine that the greatest happiness of the greatest number should be the criterion of the virtue of action

Zarathustra, (*Thus Spoke Zarathustra: A Book for All and None*), a philosophical novel by German philosopher Friedrich Nietzsche, composed in four parts written and published between 1883 and 1885.

www.ingramcontent.com/pod-product-compliance
Lightning Source LLC
Chambersburg PA
CBHW032052020426
42335CB00011B/298